The Beverly Cleary Handbook

The Beverly Cleary Handbook

Joanne Kelly

Illustrations and Maps
by
Pat Martin

Photographs
by
Charles Kelly

1996
TEACHER IDEAS PRESS
A Division of
Libraries Unlimited, Inc.
Englewood, Colorado

For Karen, Chris, and Colin.

Teacher Ideas Press
A Division of
Libraries Unlimited, Inc.
P.O. Box 6633
Englewood, CO 80155-6633
1-800-237-6124

Production Editor: Kevin W. Perizzolo
Copy Editor: Jason Cook
Proofreader: Natalie Jaro
Design and Layout: Pamela J. Getchell

Library of Congress Cataloging-in-Publication Data

Kelly, Joanne, 1934-
    The Beverly Cleary handbook / Joanne Kelly ; illustrations and
maps by Pat Martin ; photographs by Charles Kelly.
    xii, 163 p. 22x28 cm.
    Includes bibliographical references and index.
    ISBN 1-56308-245-4
    1. Cleary, Beverly--Study and teaching--Handbooks, manuals, etc.
2. Children's stories, American--Study and teaching--Handbooks,
manuals, etc. 3. Women authors, American--20th century--Biography--
Handbooks, manuals, etc. 4. Children's stories--Authorship--
Handbooks, manuals, etc.   I. Title.
PS3553.L3914Z75   1996
813'.54--dc20   96-12950
                                                              CIP

Contents

Preface ix

Introduction xi

1—About Beverly Cleary 1
Background 1
Yamhill 1
Early Years in Portland 2
Middle Years in Portland 3
High School Years 3
College and Beyond 4
Notes 5

2—Books by Beverly Cleary 6
The Portland Books 6
  Henry Huggins 7
  Henry and Beezus 8
  Henry and Ribsy 9
  Beezus and Ramona 10
  Henry and the Paper Route 11
  Henry and the Clubhouse 12
  Ribsy 14
  Ramona the Pest 15
  Ramona the Brave 16
  Ramona and Her Father 18
  Ramona and Her Mother 19
  Ramona Quimby, Age 8 21
  Ramona Forever 22
  Ellen Tebbits 25
  Otis Spofford 27
The California Books 29
  Dear Mr. Henshaw 29
  Strider 30
  The Mouse and the Motorcycle 32
  Runaway Ralph 33
  Ralph S. Mouse 35
Books for Young Readers 36
  The Growing Up Feet 36
  Hullabaloo ABC 37
  Janet's Thingamajigs 37
  Lucky Chuck 37
  Petey's Bedtime Story 38
  The Real Hole 38
  Two Dog Biscuits 38

2—Books by Beverly Cleary (continued)

More Books for Middle-Grade Readers 39
    Emily's Runaway Imagination 39
    Mitch and Amy 41
    Muggie Maggie 42
    Socks 42
Books for Older Readers 43
    Fifteen 43
    Jean and Johnny 44
    The Luckiest Girl 45
    Sister of the Bride 46
Her Own Story 47
    A Girl from Yamhill: A Memoir 47
    My Own Two Feet: A Memoir 47
Notes 48

3—Settings for Books by Beverly Cleary 49

Portland, Oregon 49
    The City and Its History 49
    Portland Today 51
    Beverly Cleary's Portland 51
Good-Bye Portland, Hello California 60
    Berkeley, California 61
    The Monterey Peninsula, California 61
Henry, Ramona, and Ribsy on Display in Their Hometown 62

4—Extended Activities 63

Projects Requiring Adult Guidance 63
    Reader's Theater 63
    Cleary Kids Bulletin Boards 69
    The Battle of Books 77
    Bookmarks and Buttons 85
Independent Activities 91
    Map Activities 91
    Hidden Names 94
    Scrambled Titles 95
    Writing Activities 96
    Activities for Individual Titles 103
    Rebuses 113
    Crossword Puzzles 119

5—Selections for Further Reading 131

Beverly Cleary's Childhood Favorites 131
    Books That Were Read Aloud to Her 131
    Books That She Read by Herself 132
Books by Beverly Cleary 133
Short Stories and Plays by Beverly Cleary 135

Nonfiction Articles by Beverly Cleary (Arranged Chronologically) 135
Articles and Books About Beverly Cleary and Her Work 138
Additional Biographical Sources 141
Notes 141

Appendix: Keys for Independent Activities (Chapter 4) 143
Index 161
About the Author 163

Preface

Beverly Cleary is, by many accounts, the most popular children's author in the United States today. Nearly every child has encountered one of her stories at some point, and many feel a sort of kinship with Ramona, Ralph, and Henry—and with Mrs. Cleary herself. Her stories are timeless and so popular with middle-grade youngsters that teachers and librarians looking for good books to read aloud will confidently turn to a Cleary book, knowing it will be greeted enthusiastically by students. This handbook provides teachers and librarians with grist for their mills. Background information about the author and her books is provided for teachers and librarians so that they can help children come to know these classic stories and increase their enjoyment and understanding. Materials are furnished for students— some to use on their own and some that will require teacher guidance. These readings and activities are designed to help students gain increased meaning and pleasure from Cleary books and to encourage students in sharing their feelings and experiences relating to the stories and characters.

Six years ago, while planning a family vacation to the Pacific Northwest, I purposefully built a day in Portland into our itinerary. What school librarian could come here and not take a ride down Klickitat Street, home of Henry Huggins and Beezus and Ramona Quimby? As we drove up and down the street, I videotaped houses, schools, and even a cat that looked like Picky-picky. I hoped to bring back the flavor of the neighborhood to a few Illinois children. I mentioned the name Beverly Cleary to the owner of a bed and breakfast and a few other local people we met, but found only blank faces staring back at me. I realize now that I just was not asking the right people.

The following school year, I shared my amateur video of Klickitat Street with a group of third-graders doing independent study on Cleary. One of them suggested that we write to the children of the school on my video, so we searched, frame by frame, until we were able to read the name above the school's door. Then a bit of research at the public library led to the correct street address, and my students composed their letter to the third-graders at the Alameda School. Did these Portland children know, we wondered, that they were receiving their education on a very famous street?

We soon found out that indeed they did! A response was in our hands within a week, and that letter was a treasure. It told of a visit by Mrs. Cleary herself (we were very impressed), and included a map of the area showing the sites of episodes from her books. That inspired my students to further their research and understanding. It turned out to be an exciting, rewarding, and educational project, in addition to being lots of fun.

Several years later I met Heather Johnson, the co-chair of the Friends of Henry and Ramona Committee, and she graciously led me to all those fascinating Portland places in Henry Huggins's neighborhood. It was a thrilling day for a long-time Cleary fan, and I am truly grateful to Mrs. Johnson for the information she has provided and for her interest and encouragement.

Thanks also to the girls and boys in Mrs. Pratt's and Mrs. Grabow's 1995–96 classes at the Thomas Paine School in Urbana, Illinois. They tested the activities in this book to make sure they were workable. I appreciate their helpful comments. Special thanks to Erin Tracey, Courtney Tamimie, Phoebe Ryan, and Elyse Michaels. To paraphrase Ramona, "I can't believe they did the whole thing!"

Introduction

The first two chapters of this book are intended for use by teachers and librarians. Chapter 1 provides background information on Beverly Cleary. Her life experiences are closely intertwined with her stories; knowledge of one increases understanding of the other. Mrs. Cleary has written such a vast array of good children's books that it would be a formidable task to keep the plots of each of them constantly in mind without confusing the episodes from one book with those of another. Chapter 2 provides detailed book summaries and notes as a ready reference source and as a survey of the breadth of her work.

Chapter 3 is designed to be read by Cleary readers of all ages. It presents a biography of the author while describing the settings for her books, all of which are places where she lived. In this chapter readers will see actual settings for episodes in the Portland stories, and they will learn bits of information, like the fact that the model for Henry's house is the former home of Cleary's girlhood friend.

Chapter 4, the activity section of this book, is divided into two parts: activities students can successfully do on their own and activities that will require guidance. Included in the latter section are some activities that require knowledge of many books by Cleary. These are intended for use by small groups of students who have read a variety of Cleary books. Working cooperatively, students can supply all the information required for the activity. It might be advisable to have a supply of books on hand for those activities. Students may want to refer to them and check out one or two they have not yet read.

It is recommended that activities not be assigned for every book that students read. If they truly enjoy a book, they will take pleasure from doing something related to the book. Allow them the freedom to decide whether to do an extended activity of their own creation, one provided here, or none at all. Students may be anxious to get on with *reading* the series—if so, a culminating activity after each series might be more appropriate than an extended activity after each book.

Mrs. Cleary receives hundreds of letters every day from both children and adults. She has made it clear that she cannot respond to children's letters prompted by classroom assignments.[1]

For those who are interested in further information about Mrs. Cleary, chapter 5 provides annotated bibliographies of books and journal articles both by and about her. Of particular interest is a listing of those books she read and enjoyed as a child. Cleary fans will enjoy sampling some of them. Answers for all the chapter 4 activities are given in the appendix.

NOTES

1. Beverly Cleary, "Dear Author, Answer This Letter Now . . ." *Instructor* 95 (November/December 1985): 22–23+.

About Beverly Cleary

Chapter One

BACKGROUND

Long before Beverly Cleary was born, forces were at work that would shape her character and the circumstances of her childhood. "Remember your pioneer ancestors" was a phrase her mother employed to prod Beverly to be courageous in the face of adversity, and even her father occasionally reminded her that her forbears had overcome hardship with vitality and determination. A teenage Beverly was later to resent the frequent references to those hardy souls who established rules of conduct that became the behavior standards for generations of their descendants.[1] Those Hawn and Bunn ancestors on her father's side of the family had indeed been brave pioneers, traveling across the United States from New York and Tennessee in 1843 and 1851. They later became reputable families in Oregon who, in addition to leaving to their children their flawless reputations, also left the Yamhill home and farm where Beverly spent the earliest years of her life.

Beverly's mother, Mable Atlee Bunn, was a young school teacher from Michigan who, in 1905, traveled to the state of Washington in search of a teaching position and adventure. Her parents followed a few years later and bought a general merchandise store in Banks, Oregon. It was while visiting with her family that she met Lloyd Bunn, a young farmer from Yamhill, Oregon. They were soon married. On April 12, 1916 Beverly Bunn was born. Cleary describes her mother as a vibrant, bright woman who was central to her development. Their relationship is a major theme of Cleary's autobiography, *A Girl from Yamhill*.

YAMHILL

Although biographies of Beverly Bunn Cleary correctly list McMinnville, Oregon as her birthplace, this fact is misleading because her mother was there, in the hospital closest to Yamhill, only to have her first baby. The 13-room house on the 80-acre Bunn farm was home for Beverly for the nearly idyllic first six years of her life. Yamhill had a population of only 366 at that time, and Beverly's family was important in the town. Her uncle was the mayor, her mother started the library, and her father was on the town council. She rode in the Fourth of July parade and was a flower girl on May Day. Her life was exceptionally happy, and she had no doubt that everyone loved her.[2]

It was during this time that Beverly's love of stories began. Although there were only three books in the house, her mother recited poetry and told stories to entertain her daughter. The stories were sometimes from her own experiences as a teacher in a one-room schoolhouse where high value was placed on reading and books. Cleary describes her mother as an independent, determined, vivacious, and intense woman who had unshakable faith in the importance of books, reading, and libraries.[3]

Yet, books were scarce in Yamhill, so her mother found time to arrange for deposits of books to be sent from the state library. Each week she spent a day acting as librarian in the makeshift library housed in an old clubroom over a bank.[4] So the first public library in Yamhill, Oregon was established, and the event provided the plot for *Emily's Runaway Imagination* (Morrow, 1961). Beverly was delighted to find that the state library provided good books for boys and girls. The stories she found there heightened her interest in learning to read, and she could not wait to begin school.[5]

EARLY YEARS IN PORTLAND

All Beverly's childhood experiences in Yamhill led her to believe that adults loved children, and that the world was, on the whole, a safe and happy place. Then hard times on the farm caused her parents to move to Portland, where Mr. Bunn would be able to find higher paying employment, and where there would be more educational advantages for Beverly. Six-year-old Beverly looked forward to playing with children and to a library full of books, which she would soon learn to read.

The family rented a six-room house, Mr. Bunn went to work as a night watchman at a bank, and Beverly had a wonderful time making friends with the neighborhood children. At last, the day she had been longing for arrived; she began first grade at the Fernwood School. The experiences this bright and eager youngster had in first grade were pivotal to her childhood and her personality—the first grade was the most terrible year of her life.

An unkind teacher was unsympathetic to the plight of this child, so used to the freedom of the country, who had come to school expecting to learn to read. There were three classroom reading groups—the Bluebirds, the Redbirds, and the Blackbirds. After illness caused her to be absent from school for several days, Beverly found herself a Blackbird, and in disgrace, wanting to read but bored and baffled by phonics lists and word drills. Once the teacher even switched her hands with a metal-tipped pointer because she was not paying attention. Beverly found her reading textbook, called a "primer", as useless as her teacher. The characters were not like any children she knew, and even the animals were unrealistically depicted. She was bored and desperately wanted a story with action. To this day, Cleary still has her copy of this hated primer with pages that are wrinkled and tear-stained.[6]

Though Beverly did eventually learn to read in second grade, it was not until third grade that she really learned to love reading books. Those dreadful first-grade experiences changed her from a lively, outgoing child to a shy little girl. Cleary says that she became a quiet, observant child because she was afraid of doing something wrong in school.[7] She developed a point of view that colored her perceptions and her writing as an adult. They would, in turn, influence the understandings of the readers of her books as she presented the insight of a Blackbird who took wing. Ramona Quimby, Otis Spofford, and Mitch in *Mitch and Amy* are all characters who encounter problems adjusting to school.

The Bunns moved to a new house in a nearby neighborhood when Beverly entered third grade, and Mr. Bunn became the lobby officer for a new bank. After a rather unhappy year, they moved again, this time just half a block from Fernwood School—close to the Rose City Branch Library and the new Hollywood Theater. By now, Beverly had overcome her reading handicap and had become an avid reader of all kinds of books. Though she enjoyed fairy tales, what she really wanted to read were stories where children could solve problems by themselves. She resented stories where children reformed at the end, or were left money by long-lost relatives, or were discovered to be the lord of the manor or heir to a fortune. Things like that did not happen to the children she knew.[8]

MIDDLE YEARS IN PORTLAND

Money was always scarce in the Bunn household, and Beverly's mother took every opportunity to save, as did most housewives of the day. Inflation in the late 1920s brought tighter budgets, and Mother began selling magazine subscriptions by telephone. Still, enough money was scraped together to send Beverly to summer camp for a week and to give her piano lessons. During these tense, depressing days, Beverly found comfort and consolation in books she borrowed from the public library. When times became too desperate, the Bunns sold their farm in Yamhill. With the proceeds, the family bought their first car and, in 1928, a home of their own.

An experience in seventh grade gave Beverly a new direction to her life. In response to a class assignment, she wrote a story about a girl who met and talked to her favorite book characters. The tale so impressed her teacher/librarian that she read it aloud to the class and commented, "When Beverly grows up, she should write children's books." Beverly was delighted and rushed home to tell her mother the astonishing news. In her usual, practical way, Mrs. Bunn responded that if her daughter intended on a writing career, she would need to have a steady way of earning a living too. It did not take Beverly very long to decide that she would someday become a librarian.

Many years later, in 1974, Cleary produced a play for National Children's Bookweek. It was entitled *The Sausage on the End of the Nose* and was published by the Children's Book Council. Interestingly, the story is about book characters such as Paddington, Homer Price, Mary Poppins, and Ramona who come to life and talk to a boy, who proudly announces that he is a non-reader![9]

HIGH SCHOOL YEARS

During Beverly's high school years, the family endured an agonizing period when Mr. Bunn, like many other men during those depression days, was unemployed. Beverly's dream of a college education seemed unattainable even after her father was able to find work. Although she was a diligent and talented student, there was simply no money to spare. Then a letter arrived from a relative in Ontario, California, who offered Beverly a place to live so she could attend the local junior college. California junior colleges charged no tuition, so the only expense would be her bus fare, which was supplied by her grandfather Atlee.

COLLEGE AND BEYOND

Unlike many girls of her day, Beverly did not attend college to catch a husband but to become independent. She wanted to become a children's librarian, the next best thing to being a writer. After graduating from Chaffee Junior College in Ontario, California, she went to the University of California at Berkeley, receiving a Bachelor of Arts degree in English in 1938. Cleary tells of an incident during those years when she was required to write an essay on "Plato, Teacher or Theorist." The paper had to be 24 pages long, but she struggled to find 24 pages of things to write on the topic. Everyone else was out enjoying the beauty of Berkeley in the spring, but she was still trying to stretch her writing. At last she resorted to wide margins and well-placed footnotes to achieve the required length. Since then, Cleary has always thought little of writing tasks of a prescribed length.

In 1939 Beverly graduated from the University of Washington library school in Seattle. Cleary well remembers her time there—it was mostly cold and windy and, because it was during the depression, all the students were experiencing tight finances. In 1975 the UW School of Library and Information Science named Cleary its Distinguished Alumna of the Year.[10]

After graduation from library school, Beverly moved to Yakima, Washington, where she was a children's librarian at the Yakima Public Library. She was young and nervous, but filled with a librarian's enthusiasm for finding the right book for the right child. A teacher at a local school asked if she might send a group of boys to the library once a week for help in selecting books that would stimulate them to read. Though Cleary eagerly accepted the challenge these lively, unenthusiastic readers presented, she soon found that she had little to offer in the way of books that appealed to children. They wanted funny books, just as she had wanted as a child, but they rejected the folktales she offered them in desperation. She remembered her own childhood frustration when looking for books about ordinary children doing ordinary kinds of things. The quantity of historical fiction dealing with the settling of the West in contrast to the lack of funny stories puzzled her. She would remember that lack of appropriate literature for ordinary children when she started writing books herself a few years later.

Another group of Yakima children influenced Beverly's future writing career. Her story-hour audience was loyal and attentive. When she began writing books, she remembered that Saturday afternoon story-hour audience and mentally told the stories to them. Then she wrote down these stories as she would have told them.[11]

In 1940 Beverly was married to Clarence T. Cleary, whom she had met in college. She gave up her job in Yakima when the young couple moved to Oakland, California. There she served as the Post Librarian at the Oakland Army Hospital during World War II, from 1942 through 1945.[12] After the war, the Clearys bought a home in the Berkeley Hills. Shortly after that, Beverly worked for several months during the Christmas rush selling children's books in a large bookstore. There she found a full range of recently published children's books, not just those selected from favorable reviews that she had encountered in her years as a librarian. Somewhat dismayed at the selection in the store, she was sure she could write a better book. After Christmas she realized that, for the first time in her life, she had free time and a quiet place to work, at an old kitchen table that had been stored in an empty bedroom of her house.

The final impetus for writing came with the discovery of several reams of typing paper left in her house by the previous owners. Now she could write a book if only she had some sharp pencils, she told her husband. The next day he brought home a pencil sharpener and Beverly decided that, if she was ever going to write a book, this was the time to do it. On January 2, 1949 she sat down to write and, in two months, she had a book about Henry Huggins and his dog, Ribsy. She sent it off to William Morrow and Company because she had heard that they were kind to authors. *Henry Huggins* was immediately accepted for publication. Thus Cleary began a long career as America's favorite author for children.

When twins Marianne Elizabeth and Malcolm James were born in 1955, finding time for writing became more difficult for Cleary.[13] In spite of the fact that raising twins was an amazingly trying job, she produced nearly one book a year for the next 25 years. Often the experiences of her children provided inspiration, and several of her books for preschoolers are based on funny happenings in the lives of her twins. For the most part, however, Cleary's memories of her own childhood in a middle-class neighborhood in Portland, Oregon have been the basis for the stories she writes. Her sharp recollections of the complex feelings of childhood and her ability to relate those feelings in a way that is both humorous and comforting to the reader make her work ever popular with children and adults.

Cleary's fans now stretch over two generations—her books have been in print for more than 40 years. During that time, her work has garnered nearly every honor available to an author of children's literature, including the prestigious Newbery Award, Regina Medal, and Laura Ingalls Wilder Award. Today Cleary's writing pace has slowed somewhat and she lives with her husband in a condominium in Carmel, California, a city that has been their home for many years. Her great desire to foster a love of reading in youngsters has not dimmed since she first became a librarian in Yakima. In 1993 Mrs. Cleary donated a large bookmobile equipped with the latest in technology to the Monterey County (California) Free Libraries so that good books would be available to children living in the most remote areas of the county.[14]

NOTES

1. Beverly Cleary, *A Girl from Yamhill: A Memoir* (New York: Morrow, 1988), 11.

2. Beverly Cleary, "Laura Ingalls Wilder Award Acceptance," *Horn Book* 51 (August 1975): 361–64.

3. Beverly Cleary, "Newbery Medal Acceptance," *Horn Book* 60 (August 1984): 430.

4. Beverly Cleary, "Writing Books About Henry Huggins," *Top of the News* 24 (December 1957): 7.

5. Beverly Cleary, "How Long Does It Take to Write a Book?" *Oklahoma Librarian* 21 (July 1971): 16.

6. Beverly Cleary, "On Talking Back to Authors," *Claremond Reading Conference Yearbook* 34 (1970): 3.

7. David Reuther, "Beverly Cleary," *Horn Book* 60 (August 1984): 440.

8. Beverly Cleary, "Beverly Cleary—1980 Regina Medal Recipient (Acceptance Speech)," *Catholic Library World* 52 (July 1980): 23.

9. Beverly Cleary, *The Sausage on the End of the Nose* (New York: Children's Book Council, 1974).

10. Jean Reichenbach, "Beverly Cleary," *Columns: The University of Washington Alumni Journal* (September 1993): 41.

11. Shirley Fitzgibbons, "A National Heroine and International Favorite: Focus on Beverly Cleary," *Top of the News* 37 (Winter 1977): 168.

12. *Contemporary Authors: New Revision Series*, vol. 36 (Detroit: Gale, 1992), 87.

13. Ilene Cooper, "The Booklist Interview: Beverly Cleary," *Booklist* 87 (October 15, 1990): 448.

14. "Cleary Donates Bookmobile Gift," *Wilson Library Bulletin* (September 1993): 18.

Chapter Two

Books by Beverly Cleary

THE PORTLAND BOOKS

Portland, Oregon is the setting for the *Henry Huggins* and *Ramona Quimby* books, and for *Otis Spofford* and *Ellen Tebbits*. The Portland stories are the most popular of Beverly Cleary's works. In them she has provided books for those average children who want stories about boys and girls who have experiences and feelings similar to their own—funny stories that do not appear "babyish" yet have formats that are not threatening for neophyte readers. Cleary's own frightful school experiences are reflected in Ramona's unhappy times in the primary grades. The author has a special compassion for children who have difficulty conforming and learning.

The first of the Portland stories, *Henry Huggins*, was written in 1950 and the last, *Ramona Forever*, in 1984. Though 34 years may have passed as we measure time, time passes at a more leisurely pace in Henry and Ramona's neighborhood. Ramona is but a three-year-old in *Henry Huggins*; in *Ramona Forever* she is in the third grade.

Careful reading will reveal that changes in middle-class American life that occurred during the last 34 years are reflected in the novels. Television is seldom mentioned in the early books about Henry, but it has become a strong influence by the time Ramona tries to think of ways to ease the family's financial crisis in *Ramona and Her Father*—she dreams of being a star of television commercials.

With the exception of Valerie Spofford, all the mothers in the early novels stayed at home and kept house for their families. When Mrs. Quimby gets a job in a doctor's office in *Ramona the Brave*, she is reflecting the trend for women of the 1970s. Her job becomes full-time when Father loses his job in *Ramona and Her Father*, and the children feel the stresses and strains brought to a family by this situation. Ramona is unhappy with the after-school daycare at Howie's house; Mr. Quimby shows symptoms of depression; and, in *Ramona and Her Mother*, Beezus turns into a temperamental teenager, Mother and Father argue, and the girls worry about divorce. Cleary writes for the children of middle-class families, and her stories chronicle the changing concerns of these children as they cope with modern society.

The Portland novels are episodic, that is, each chapter is a complete story within itself, and common threads of concern link all the chapters within a book. When, in *Ramona and Her Father*, Mr. Quimby is unemployed and his daughters want him to stop smoking, these unresolved concerns surface throughout the novel until they are resolved in the last chapter. Contained within each Portland novel are other stories: Ramona gets burrs tangled in her hair, she learns how to make tin-can stilts, and Picky-picky eats the Halloween jack-o'-lantern that Father has so carefully carved.

As readers share their enjoyment of these stories, they will naturally refer to individual episodes within the books that are especially appealing to them. Provided here are detailed summaries to facilitate locating individual episodes. However, a summary cannot possibly convey the wonderful humor and keen perceptions Cleary has woven into her stories.

Henry Huggins

(New York: Morrow, 1950)
Illustrated by Louis Darling

Henry is a normal and natural third-grader who earnestly wants to do the right thing—most of the time. He befriends a stray dog he comes upon in a drug store and names him Ribsy because his ribs show through his skin. Henry's mom cannot come downtown to pick him up, but she suggests that he bring his new pet home on the city bus. Dogs are not allowed on the city buses unless they are confined in a box, so Henry, lacking a suitable box, settles on a shopping bag. Mayhem erupts when Ribsy escapes from the bag and races up the aisle, upsetting other riders and their packages. The police arrive looking for Henry and, to his delight, they drive him home.

Henry has an interesting assortment of friends and neighbors who live on Klickitat Street. There is his good old friend Robert, and there is Scooter McCarthy, who is two years older than Henry and whom Henry envies and admires. Henry enjoys the company of Beezus Quimby, a sensible girl, but her tag along little sister Ramona annoys him with her fantastic imagination and her determination to be the center of attention.

Henry buys a pair of guppies on sale at the pet store. He has no idea that, because of the speedy reproductive habits of the fish, he will soon have so many guppies that he will not even be able to give them all away in the neighborhood. Still, he gamely spends most of his spare time caring for his ever growing brood, which soon occupies all his mother's canning jars. The situation reaches a crisis stage when canning season approaches and he must return the jars.

Henry's parents are patient, understanding, and supportive, but not indulgent. When Henry is responsible for replacing a lost football, they do not offer to pay for a new one. However, when Henry sets out to earn the money by catching 1,331 nightcrawlers in Grant Park in one evening, his parents pitch in to help him capture the last 228.

Ribsy and Henry are inseparable. Together they meet with a hilarious series of adventures. Ribsy saves Henry from the humiliating part of a little boy in the school Christmas program when the dog tips over a can of green paint. It drenches and dyes Henry, and he must play a green elf instead. Ribsy nearly disgraces himself and Henry by his unconventional appearance and behavior during a pet show in the park. Then Ribsy saves the day by being named the most unusual dog in the show.

When a strange boy shows up, claiming to be Ribsy's real owner, Henry is in serious trouble. He wants to be fair, but he cannot bear the thought of giving up Ribsy. With the help of his friends, he manages a realistic, heartwarming solution.

♦ *Henry Huggins* received the New England Round Table of Children's Librarians Honor Award in 1972.

Henry and Beezus

(New York: Morrow, 1952)
Illustrated by Louis Darling

Although Beezus is a girl—and Henry does not think much of girls—he does consider her to be unusually sensible and especially helpful. The trouble is that her pesky little sister Ramona is always in the way and always playing dumb games. Henry considers Robert to be his best friend among the children on Klickitat Street, and Scooter McCarthy, the neighborhood bully and tease, is Henry's worst enemy. Among other irritations, Scooter is always showing off on his new bike. For example, there is a scene in which Ribsy snatches a beef roast from a neighbor's barbecue pit. Even though Henry races down the street after his dog, it is Scooter who rescues the roast by chasing down Ribsy on his bike, and it is Henry who gets in trouble.

The thing that Henry wants most in the world is the beautiful red bike in the window of the Rose City Bike and Trike Shop. Unfortunately, his parents cannot afford to buy it for him, so Henry explores ways to earn the money himself. Beezus, in spite of her sister Ramona, is the one Henry turns to when he needs help to work out his schemes.

He believes he has found instant wealth when he discovers 49 boxes of bubble gum in an empty lot. Why not sell them to the kids at school? At first, sales are brisk, but business fades after several days. When the school principal explains to everyone why chewing gum is not a good idea, it is Beezus who helps Henry get rid of his treasure.

Next, Henry tries to earn money by being a substitute paper boy. Ribsy seriously handicaps him by retrieving every paper delivered on Klickitat Street and returning them to the Huggins's front porch. It is Ramona with her squirt gun who suggests a solution to this predicament.

Desperate for a bike, Henry goes to an auction at the police station, hoping to find a bike in reasonable condition costing four dollars and four cents, or less. Beezus offers to help, but of course Ramona must tag along. Things get complicated when Ribsy gets a parking ticket and Ramona, tired of the crowd at the auction, loudly announces that she is going to throw up. Still, with Beezus's help, Henry makes a successful bid, but only to discover that he has spent all his money for a girl's bike.

Henry and his parents go to the grand opening of the Colossal Market. He and his friends enjoy free samples and sign up for door prizes. Henry hears his name announced as the winner of a prize, but his excitement turns to disgust when he discovers, to the amusement of the crowd, that he has won fifty dollars worth of free service at a ladies beauty salon. It is Beezus who suggests the wonderful solution that ultimately leads to the glorious day when Henry, on his sparkling red bike, triumphantly pedals past Scooter's house.

Henry and Ribsy

(New York: Morrow, 1954)

Illustrated by Louis Darling

It is late summer, and Henry still considers Ribsy to be "the best dog there is," but few of the neighbors agree. Ribsy runs through lawns, chases cats, and generally makes a nuisance of himself. After a particularly embarrassing incident in which Ribsy makes off with a policeman's lunch bag, Mr. Huggins makes a bargain with Henry: if Henry will keep Ribsy out of trouble until the middle of September, he may accompany his dad on a salmon fishing trip. Henry agrees but, recalling Ribsy's past mishaps, doubts that he can keep Ribsy out of trouble for long.

Henry increases his allowance by undertaking the daily job of emptying the kitchen garbage into the trash can outside the house. Ribsy growls and barks at the garbage collector, and the man has to retreat without emptying the Huggins's can. Henry cannot understand his normally good-natured pet's reaction until he discovers that Ribsy considers himself to be a guard dog. He is determined to protect *all* his master's possessions, including Henry's "precious garbage," from thieves. Although Henry solves the problem, Scooter tells everyone in the neighborhood that Ribsy viciously attacked the garbage man—yet another blot on Ribsy's already spotted reputation.

After a comical episode in which Mrs. Huggins decides to save money by giving Henry haircuts at home, school finally begins. Early in September, Beezus and Henry set out to play a quiet game of checkers, but of course Ramona tags along, licking an ice cream cone. Ramona pretends that her lunch box is a camera and tries to take Henry's picture, and Ribsy snatches the ice cream. An enraged Ramona grabs Ribsy's bone and locks it inside her lunch box. The resulting hullabaloo ends up in the schoolyard with Ramona making a terrible scene from the top of the jungle gym and Ribsy barking below for his bone. Ribsy's bad reputation makes the situation even worse when the ladies from the PTA come upon the scene and assume that the dog is frightening Ramona. Henry is sure that the dog catcher will take Ribsy away and that he will lose his chance to go salmon fishing with his dad. An understanding school principal and Mrs. Huggins arrive just in time to save the day.

At last the great day arrives, and Henry and Ribsy leave before dawn for the Umptucca River to go salmon fishing with Dad and their next-door neighbor, Mr. Grumbie. Two grown men, an energetic boy, and a restless dog make for a tight fit in a small motor boat in a cold rain. The fish are not biting, lunch is eaten before ten o'clock in the morning, and things get a bit boring. Ribsy upsets the tackle box, shakes water in everyone's lunch, then leaps into the water, causing Mr. Grumbie to lose a giant salmon. After a struggle, a cold and soggy dog is lifted back into the boat, and Ribsy and Henry are deposited back at the dock to dry off. Henry is sure that he has lost his chance to catch a salmon.

Henry and Ribsy explore the shoreline where the river empties into the Pacific Ocean while they wait for Dad and Mr. Grumbie. Ribsy's barking attracts Henry, who discovers a large Chinook salmon swimming up a tiny stream. Henry desperately searches for a way to catch the fish, finally jumping into the chilly water to grab it. The fish fights, but Henry struggles. He manages to get a firm hold but finds that the fish is too heavy. Ribsy's barking attracts a fisherman who helps land the salmon, and Henry triumphantly returns to the boathouse, staggering under the weight of the fish. The salmon weighs in at 29 pounds, impressing all the men at the scales. Best of all, just as Henry is having his picture taken with his catch, who should walk by but Scooter McCarthy, who fished all day but did not catch anything. To Henry's credit, he does feel a pang of sympathy for Scooter, but that does not dim his joy and pride.

♦ *Henry and Ribsy* received the Pacific Northwest Library Association Young Reader's Choice Award in 1957.

Beezus and Ramona

(New York: Morrow, 1955)
Illustrated by Louis Darling

Beezus is nine, and four-year-old Ramona goes to nursery school. Ramona's favorite book is about Scoopy, the littlest steam shovel. The family tires of reading *Scoopy* to Ramona, who always fills in all the sound effects at the top of her lungs. She pesters long-suffering Beezus until Beezus has a happy inspiration and takes Ramona to the library to find another book. Ramona does not understand libraries; she is noisy when she should be quiet, demands a library card of her own when she cannot even write her name, and generally embarrasses Beezus. She does find another favorite book about a big steam shovel named Steve.

The day arrives to return *Big Steve* to the library, but Ramona claims that the book is hers and it cannot be returned. She scribbles on every page in purple crayon to prove it. A shamefaced Beezus pays the librarian for the damage, and the librarian explains to Ramona that the book belongs to Beezus now. Beezus tells Ramona that she will read the book to her only when *she* feels like it.

Beezus attends an after-school art class at Glenwood Park on Fridays, and Ramona must play nearby in the sandpile. Beezus wants to please her instructor but feels that she has no imagination, unlike her sister. Ramona walks into the class, and the teacher not only allows her to stay, but sets her up with an easel and brush next to Beezus. Quickly tiring of painting, Ramona soon disrupts the class, so Beezus firmly sends her back to the sandpile. Somehow the incident has inspired Beezus: she decides to paint Ramona's imaginary lizard, Ralph. Her version of Ralph is a wonderful dragon, which receives lavish praise from her teacher.

One day Beezus and Henry are trying to play a few quiet games of checkers, but Ramona pesters them constantly. She tips over the checkerboard, throws a tantrum, is sent to her room, and puts Ribsy in the Quimby bathroom, where he scratches at the door in a panic, accidentally locking himself inside. Mrs. Quimby is able to unlock the door with a nail file and free Ribsy. Henry decides that it is time to take his dog and go home. Beezus is exasperated with her little sister, but uncomfortable with her hateful feelings, particularly when she considers the close relationship Mrs. Quimby has with her sister, Beatrice.

One day, while Beezus is baby-sitting for Mother, Ramona hides. She is in the basement going through a box of apples, taking just one bite out of each because "The first bite tastes best." Horrified at the waste of good food, Beezus angrily scolds her sister. Aunt Beatrice, who is a fourth-grade teacher, hears the sad story on the phone and suggests that Beezus ignore Ramona's bad behavior and make applesauce instead. Mother and Father agree to follow that advice, but Beezus is doubtful that she will ever feel better about her little sister.

Things get even worse on a rainy Saturday just after the girls have washed their hair. Sixteen or more (she never could get an exact count) soggy little children in wet boots shock Beezus when they stomp up the front steps. Ramona has invited her nursery school class to a party, but has neglected to tell her family. Beezus and her mother quickly improvise entertainment and refreshments. At last, a reason for all that applesauce! The children finally go home after a parade, warm cookies, and a tantrum from Ramona. Beezus helps her mother clean up and learns that, as children, Mother and Aunt Beatrice were as different as Beezus and Ramona.

On the day that Beezus is 10 years old, she happily anticipates having Aunt Beatrice join them for her birthday dinner. After Ramona manages to cause the failure of two birthday cakes, Beezus decides that she really does not love her sister. Aunt Beatrice arrives with a third cake, and the birthday dinner is off to a successful start, but Ramona is asked to leave the table because of her misbehavior. Mother and Aunt Beatrice begin to reminisce about their childhood and laugh about how much trouble they caused for each other. They readily admit that there were many times they did not love each other, but their shared affection now is unmistakable. With relief, Beezus is able to conclude that it is natural to dislike your sister from time to time, and this understanding makes Ramona seem a bit less exasperating to Beezus.

Henry and the Paper Route

(New York: Morrow, 1957)

Illustrated by Louis Darling

Henry, a ten-year-old fifth-grader at the Glenwood School, is not quite old enough to have a paper route. He admires the way Scooter rides down Klickitat Street, tossing *Journals* on the porches of subscribers.

In his first attempt to talk to the man in charge of local paper routes, four squirmy kittens plague Henry. He bought them at a rummage sale along the way and has them hidden in his jacket. Kindly Mr. Capper advises Henry to apply again when he is a few years older.

Henry resolves to prove to Mr. Capper that he is capable of handling a route, and to do so he will sell subscriptions to the *Journal* to all the neighbors. He even offers a free kitten as a premium to each new subscriber. Not only does he not sell any subscriptions, he cannot find homes for the kittens either, so he gives his four tiny orphans to Mr. Pennycuff, the owner of the pet store. Later, Mr. Huggins finds that he misses his favorite kitten, so he gives Henry the money to buy him back again, and even Henry's dog Ribsy is happy about that.

The same day that Scooter asks Henry to fold and deliver his papers, there is an announcement about an upcoming school paper drive. Classes at Glenwood School will collect old newspapers as a fund raiser—the class collecting the most papers wins a prize. Henry has an inspiration: in every paper he delivers for Scooter, he includes a notice announcing the paper drive and giving his name and phone number for pickup. The plan backfires. The response to Henry's advertisement is overwhelming, and Scooter is angry. Again Beezus comes to Henry's aid. With Ramona (who is pretending to be a monkey) tagging along, Beezus helps Henry collect all the newspapers. The garage is filled with newspapers that must be bundled and delivered to the school.

After days of work, and with the help of his friends and his mom and dad, Henry completes his task, and his class handily wins the contest.

Finally, on his eleventh birthday, Henry is old enough to have a paper route. A few days later, Scooter comes down with the chicken pox, and Henry is asked to take over until Scooter is well. Henry begins the job with enthusiasm, only faintly dimmed by the discovery that the new boy on the block is a genius named Murph who plays chess, is building a robot named Thorvo, and, Henry suspects, may try to get a paper route that Henry had set his sights on.

Murph fascinates Ramona, and she follows him everywhere and even begins wearing glasses (without the glass) so that she will look like him. Murph does get the route Henry wanted, but Ramona causes so much trouble for him that he gives up and relinquishes the paper route to a very surprised and delighted Henry. However, Henry is wary of Ramona, who brought down the neighborhood genius.

Ramona begins playing tricks on Henry, and he knows that he must somehow outwit her. With a burst of inspiration, he devises a mechanical-man costume for Ramona. He tells her that, if she wants to be a robot like Thorvo, she must walk slowly, not bending her knees or waist. Enchanted, Ramona spends her days slowly clanking up and down the sidewalk while Henry triumphantly and successfully makes the deliveries on his own paper route.

♦ *Henry and the Paper Route* received the Young Reader's Choice Award from the Pacific Northwest Library Association in 1960.

Henry and the Clubhouse

(New York: Morrow, 1962)

Illustrated by Louis Darling

Mr. Grumbie is hauling an old bathtub to the city dump, and he asks Henry if he would like to go along and ride in the bathtub. Only when they are amid all the traffic on busy Lombard Street does Henry remember his paper route. He knows that he will never make it to Mr. Capper's house on time, so he leaves Mr. Grumbie, telephones his mom, and searches for a bus that can get him home. While riding what seems to be the world's slowest bus, Henry spots his mom delivering the papers on his route. She is a terrible thrower, but Henry realizes that she has saved his job. He feels guilty even before his father sternly explains about the responsibility that must be a part of having a paper route.

A windfall in the form of lumber and other building material comes Henry's way when a neighbor builds a new garage and tears down the old one. Henry and his friends Robert and Murph decide to build a clubhouse, and construction is soon underway. Henry is busier than ever and feels rather harried with the clubhouse project and trying to be a reliable newsboy.

To prove that he is a responsible newsboy, Henry plans to sell a *Journal* subscription to a new family on his route, but their dog gets into a fight with Ribsy. After that, whenever Henry ventures down that street, Ranger the dalmation is after him with teeth flashing.

Halloween finds Henry dressed up as a fierce Indian in war paint accompanied by Ribsy in a wolf mask. He meets Murph, who has made himself a man-from-outer-space outfit with eyes that light up, and they decide to go trick-or-treating. At one of their stops, a friendly woman gives Henry a stuffed owl as a treat because she does not have any candy—Henry happily plans to hang the owl in the clubhouse.

Tempted by rumors of candy apples, the boys risk a visit to Ranger's house. To their surprise, Ranger cowers under a chair, afraid of the owl Henry is carrying. However, the lady of the house is so friendly that Henry is able to sell her a subscription to the *Journal*.

Henry finds that having a paper route is not easy, and it often keeps him from working on the clubhouse with Robert and Murph. He tries to hurry when collecting subscription money, but delays hamper him. At one house, a harried mother puts him in charge of her unruly brood of children while she goes in search of her purse. Ramona, who happens to be visiting her friend Lisa (one of the brood), climbs onto the washing machine and opens it to see how it works. Dirty water sprays out, drenching the walls, the children, and the dog. In the hubbub that follows, Henry leaves without having collected his money. Disgusted with Ramona, he resolutely turns around and returns to the scene of the battle to get his money.

Murph has decided that no girls are to be allowed near the clubhouse, and although Henry feels a bit guilty about turning away Beezus, who frequently offers to help with the building, he does not argue. Beezus and Ramona are ordered to leave. Then mysterious things begin to happen at the clubhouse, and the boys, suspecting that Beezus is the cause, buy a lock to secure their place when they are away.

Ramona locks Henry inside the clubhouse and, try as he might, he cannot escape. He realizes that it is time to start his paper route and becomes desperate to find a way out. He promises Ramona that if she will unlock the door, he will teach her the secret club chant. She cannot open the lock, so Beezus comes to his aid only after he teaches her the chant, too.

Ramona continues to bother Henry on his paper route, and he tries to think of a clever way to outwit her. He writes to Sheriff Bud, the host of Ramona's favorite television show, and tells him about how she causes problems for him while he is trying to deliver his papers. To Henry's surprise, on a program a few days later, the Sheriff points his finger into television land and tells Ramona Geraldine Quimby to stop pestering Henry Huggins on his paper route! Ramona is awestruck, and Henry thinks that his troubles are over.

Unfortunately, now that Ramona thinks Henry is Sheriff Bud's friend, Henry becomes her hero and she follows him everywhere. She gets a miniature *Journal* carrier bag as a Christmas gift, and even when the city flounders under a foot of snow, she struggles on, shadowing Henry. He has a terrible time delivering papers in the snowstorm, and he tries to ignore Ramona's attempts to keep up with him. She begins to cry and looks so cold and tired that he cannot help feeling sorry for her. With Beezus's help, he loads Ramona on his sled and they take her home. Then he must go back out in the blizzard and finish his route.

Henry gets his reward when Mrs. Peabody writes a letter to the editor of the *Journal* commending him for the extra effort he gives to customers on his route and for his kindness to a little girl during the snowstorm. Mr. Capper is impressed, and Mr. Huggins is so proud that he buys copies of the paper to send to the relatives. He praises Henry for showing responsibility and gives him the five dollars he needs to buy a sleeping bag for which he has been saving. A pleased Henry thinks that, thanks to Ramona, things worked out for the best.

Ribsy

(New York: Morrow, 1964)

Illustrated by Louis Darling

The Huggins have a new car, but Ribsy is not allowed inside. On a rainy Saturday in October, the family leaves for a trip to the shopping mall. Ribsy chases the car until Mrs. Huggins relents, and Ribsy jumps inside. He is so wet that he is made to stay on the floor of the car, and Henry takes off his dog collar so he can scratch a pesky flea on his neck.

Ribsy, left alone in the car, barks frantically at another dog, and his paw hits the power window button. The window slides down, and Ribsy is free. He races jubilantly around the vast parking lot trying to find Henry, and then cannot find his way back to the car. Cold, wet, and bedraggled, he at last scrambles through the window of a car that has a familiar shape and a familiar new-car smell.

Ribsy mistakenly joins a family with a baby boy and four girls, who beg their parents to keep the new dog. They happily drive home with him, as Ribsy realizes that this is the wrong family and that they are driving away from Klickitat Street. At home, Ribsy is given a bath with violet bubble bath and is more convinced than ever that he must get back to Henry. He escapes, but he cannot get rid of the smell of violets.

Henry and his family vainly search the parking lot at the shopping center, call the Humane Society, and prepare a lost dog advertisement for the newspaper.

Ribsy, still searching for Henry, is taken in by an elderly widow who wants to dress him up and teach him tricks. He runs away from her and is soon adopted by a second-grade class. After a chaotic episode with a pet squirrel brought to the classroom for Show and Tell, Ribsy is back on the street.

Henry and his family talk to many people who answer their advertisement, including the family who gave Ribsy a bubble bath. The report disgusts Henry, but it is the only clue they have to Ribsy's whereabouts. Mr. Huggins suggests that Henry pick out another dog, but he refuses.

Ribsy's next adventure is at a high school football game, where he decides to join the boys who are running around and playing with a ball on a flat grassy field. Ribsy, who always wants to be part of the fun, trips up the quarterback, who is heading down the field for a game-winning touchdown, and he drops the ball just short of the goal line. A newspaper photographer snaps the picture, the game is over, and the crowd goes wild. A boy named Joe, with patched jeans and long hair, grabs Ribsy, telling the newspaper reporter that the dog is his.

The *Journal* prints a front-page picture and detailed article about Ribsy's football adventure. Henry Huggins calls Joe to claim the dog. Joe refuses until Henry mentions a reward. To prove that the dog is really his, Henry suggests that Joe hold the phone to Ribsy's ear so Henry can talk to him. Ribsy hears Henry's voice and becomes so excited that he dashes out the front door and down the street looking for him. Ribsy is confused and lost again to Henry's disappointment.

The next day, Ribsy makes friends with a lonely boy named Larry, who tries to take Ribsy up to his apartment on an elevator but is almost caught by a cantankerous building manager. He stuffs Ribsy out a window and onto a fire escape. Poor Ribsy, stranded outside, cannot keep his feet from slipping through the bars of the fire escape. Frightened and unable to find a way to escape, Ribsy tries to bark away his fear. Henry and his parents have been driving around in the neighborhood near Joe's house looking everywhere for Ribsy, and they finally find him stuck on the fire escape. There is a heroic rescue and a joyful reunion. Ribsy is driven home in style in the new car, and no one minds at all.

♦ *Ribsy* received the Dorothy Canfield Fisher Memorial Children's Book Award in 1961 and the Nene Award in 1968.

Ramona the Pest

(New York: Morrow, 1968)
Illustrated by Louis Darling

Ramona is five and off to kindergarten. Her goal is to learn to read and write immediately—to catch up with Beezus—but her first day is marred by misunderstanding. Young and pretty Miss Binney, Ramona's teacher, tells her to sit in a little chair "for the present." Ramona is thrilled and remains glued to her chair through all the morning activities, awaiting her reward. The misunderstanding is discovered when Miss Binney questions Ramona about why she refuses to join the class outside for recess. The day worsens when she pulls a classmate's appealing red curls and is dubbed the "worst rester" during rest time. Ramona admits to herself that although she loves her teacher, kindergarten is not what she had expected.

On the second day of school, Ramona decides to take her doll, Chevrolet, for Show and Tell. The children laugh at the doll's name, but Miss Binney thinks it is beautiful. The children laugh at Howie Kemp's ragged rabbit, too, but he does not admit that he borrowed it from Ramona. Miss Binney ties a red ribbon on the bunny. On the way home from school, Howie returns Ramona's rabbit but not the ribbon. The problem is solved when, in exchange for the ribbon, Ramona allows Howie to remove a rear wheel from her tricycle, thus converting it to a two-wheeler.

The kindergartners are learning to write their names, and Ramona is delighted to find that she has an interesting-looking name. Ramona loves Miss Binney and calls her "the nicest teacher in the whole world." It is especially upsetting then, when one day Ramona discovers that a strange woman has taken Miss Binney's place in the kindergarten. She feels that she has been deserted when she sees a substitute is sitting at Miss Binney's desk. The rest of the children enter the classroom, but Ramona hides behind some trash cans at the edge of the schoolyard until she is cold, tired, and has to go to the bathroom. She is discovered by some older children, including Henry and Beezus. Miss Mullens, the principal, understands Ramona's distress about Miss Binney and takes her back to her classroom without comment. Ramona is reconciled to the substitute but knows that this woman can never replace the beloved Miss Binney.

Ramona has new red boots, and on the next rainy day she splashes happily all the way to school. At the corner where Henry is the crossing guard, Ramona detours to the nearby construction site of a new supermarket to splash in the mud. Despite Henry's warnings, she is soon firmly stuck, unable to pull her new red boots out of the dark, heavy mud. Miss Binney rushes over to help and calls upon Henry to perform the rescue operation. He wades in and carries Ramona to safety, but her feet slip out of her boots and they are left behind. Horrified at her loss, she begins to cry, so Henry slogs back into the mud and retrieves the boots. Ramona declares loudly to the whole school that she will marry Henry Huggins.

For Halloween, Ramona is a witch with a scary rubber mask. Hidden behind that mask she can do all sorts of things, such as give Davy, her favorite boy, a kiss and pull Susan's tempting curls. Frightened by the thought that, because no one knows her, perhaps she is not Ramona anymore, she rushes into the classroom and quickly makes a sign to carry in the parade. The sign reads "RAMONA Q."

Ramona loses her first tooth at school. Everyone admires the tooth and praises Ramona for her bravery. Miss Binney agrees to keep the precious tooth in her drawer until it is time to go home, and Ramona is sure that her teacher loves her—so much so that she can get away with anything. She is exuberant and pulls Susan's curls again, not stopping even when Miss Binney tells her that she cannot come back to kindergarten until she stops pulling Susan's hair. Ramona is not sure she can stop and, although she loves kindergarten, she leaves thinking that she will never return. She even forgets her precious tooth in Miss Binney's desk drawer.

At home, things grow tense as the school situation is investigated and discussed, and another misunderstanding of words throws Ramona into a tantrum. Since the first day of school when she learned the "Star Spangled Banner," Ramona has believed that a "dawnzer" is a lamp that gives a "lee light." Discovering her error, which seems so funny to her family, is just too much for Ramona to take, and she retreats to her room and pounds her heels on the wall.

Ramona is convinced that Miss Binney dislikes her, and she resolves never to return to kindergarten. She mopes at home to the dismay of her family, who is determined to be patient. Just when Ramona despairs of ever returning to school, Miss Binney sends her a letter containing her tooth and asking when she will return to kindergarten. Finally Ramona feels that she is wanted again and can happily return to school.

♦ *Ramona the Pest* received a Pacific Northwest Library Association Young Reader's Choice Award in 1971, the Georgia Children's Award in 1970, the Nene Award in 1971, and the Sequoyah Children's Book Award in 1971.

Ramona the Brave

(New York: Morrow, 1975)

Illustrated by Alan Tiegreen

Ramona is six and about to enter first grade. She is feeling especially grown-up these days, so when some older boys in the park tease Beezus about her nickname, Ramona bravely comes to her defense. To Ramona's surprise, it turns out that Beezus does not want her help; in fact, she is embarrassed by the lecture her little sister delivers to the boys. As the tale is unfolded to Mother, Ramona becomes contrite and suggests that Beezus be called her real name, Beatrice, from now on.

Mrs. Quimby is starting a job as a part-time bookkeeper for their doctor to finance an addition on the house, so the girls will no longer have to share a bedroom. They will take turns using the new room, and Ramona, who never gets to do anything first, will have the room all to herself for the first six months.

Ramona and Howie's favorite game is Brick Factory—pounding old bricks into powder on the Quimby's driveway—a messy but satisfying procedure. Workmen begin to work on the addition. Ramona and Howie realize that, in a few days, they will be able to jump through a hole in the back of the house. Exciting as all this is, Beezus and Ramona decide that it is scary sleeping in a house with a hole in it.

Ramona has been waiting for school to begin for weeks, so that she can tell the first-graders that two men chopped a hole in her house, but when she tells the class, the children do not believe her. She calls upon Howie to confirm her story, but he denies it. Mrs. Griggs is angry, and some of the boys call Ramona a liar. Later Howie explains to her that the men did not chop a hole in her house. They pried off siding with crowbars. Ramona and Howie argue and Howie takes all his old bricks out of the Quimby garage, ending the game of Brick Factory.

First grade is not going well for Ramona because she has an easy time doing the work but a hard time remembering the rules. Susan, who always does everything just right and has those long, tempting curls, copies a paper-bag owl that Ramona has created and proudly displays it to Mrs. Griggs. Ramona knows that nobody likes a tattletale, so she does not say a word. Instead she angrily destroys her owl, but she is overcome with vengeance when Susan prepares her owl for display on the afternoon before Parent's Night. In a burst of temper, Ramona grabs Susan's owl, tears it up, and then runs home. She falls on the way and arrives home with bloodied knees and a tearstained face. Poor Ramona wants to be liked by everyone, and she cannot admit to her mother the terrible thing she has done at school.

Mr. and Mrs. Quimby leave for Parent's Night at Glenwood School, and while Beezus is eager for them to meet her wonderful new teacher, Mr. Cardoza, Ramona suffers from guilt and worry. Going to bed in her new room does not help, so she gets up and leaves a note that reads, "Come here Mother. Come here to me." When her parents return, they discuss the owl situation with her and, although they are understanding, her parents insist that Ramona apologize to Susan. Mrs. Griggs demands that Ramona make a public apology, and she ends up humiliated, angry, and even more sure that she is a misfit in school.

Ramona is learning to read, but she is unhappy at school because she is convinced that Mrs. Griggs does not like her. Mother is busier than ever because of her new job; there are scant minutes for making cookies or comforting little girls. Even Picky-picky, the family cat, dislikes Ramona and will never sit on her lap or play with her. Worst of all, Ramona feels alone and afraid of the dark in her new room, but she is ashamed to admit it—this would be as bad as admitting she was not growing up and being brave.

Mrs. Griggs passes out progress reports to take home, and Ramona dreads showing hers to her family, for she is sure that Mrs. Griggs wrote bad things about her. When Ramona finds that her progress report notes satisfactory academic progress but a lack of self-control, she flies into a rage, shouting that Mrs. Griggs is unfair and that she will say a bad word. Her family sits in shocked silence as she shouts, "Guts!" Then they laugh at her, and she goes into a full-fledged tantrum. Although her family begins to understand her frustration and unhappiness, they do not grant to Ramona's request to be moved to another class. Her parents explain that she will have to show her spunk and learn to make the best of Mrs. Griggs's first grade. Their confidence in her gives Ramona some spirit, makes her feel better about herself, and convinces her that she can even overcome her fear of the dark in her new room.

The next morning, a large, growling dog chases Ramona on her way to school and takes the shoe she hurls at him. She tries to hide her bare foot and is surprised when the children and Mrs. Griggs respond to her story with sympathy and understanding. Ramona constructs a slipper for herself out of paper towels, and Mrs. Griggs, favorably impressed with her creativity, allows Ramona to improve on the slipper while the rest of the class makes Thanksgiving turkeys. Still, Ramona worries about what her mother will say about the lost shoe, so she is relieved when the school secretary announces that the owner of the dog has returned it. The toothmarks have only slightly scarred the shoe, and the secretary praises Ramona for her bravery. Filled with self-confidence, Ramona returns to her classroom ready to face any challenge.

♦ *Ramona the Brave* received the Golden Archer Award in 1977 and the Mark Twain Award in 1978.

Ramona and Her Father

(New York: Morrow, 1975)

Illustrated by Alan Tiegreen

Ramona is happy in second grade, but Beezus does not like her sixth-grade teacher. Mother is still working part-time to pay for last year's room addition to the house, and Picky-picky is as grumpy as ever. Then a terrible thing happens, and Ramona and Beezus are confronted with a real grown-up problem. Mr. Quimby loses his job, and both parents are very concerned about the future.

Finding a new job is difficult, so Mrs. Quimby goes to work full-time while Mr. Quimby is home filling out applications and taking care of the house. Money is a big problem, and Ramona longs to help. She dreams of being one of those children in television commercials who earn millions of dollars just by being cute. Secretly she practices "cuteness," and one day fashions a crown out of burrs, pretending to be a boy in the margarine commercial. The burrs stick fast, and her father is forced to cut them out, but he reassures her that he would not trade her for any television celebrity.

Stringent economy measures are in place in the Quimby household as Father's unemployment continues. Everyone stoically endures the tight budget except Picky-picky, the cat who refuses to eat a cheaper brand of cat food. Halloween approaches and, with it, the gift of a pumpkin for the Quimbys. A wonderful evening is spent with the whole family involved in the design and carving of a fearsome jack-o-lantern. Ramona awakens in the middle of the night to find Picky-picky eating the pumpkin. Beezus flies into an angry rage, screaming that there would be enough money for good cat food if Father would only give up the cigarettes that are blackening his lungs and will kill him.

Ramona thinks action is called for, and the girls begin a no-smoking campaign on Father, and he soon loses patience with them. One day after school, Father and Ramona decide to draw the longest picture in the world, an illustrated map of Oregon. As they draw together happily, Ramona apologizes for harassing her father, and Father promises to try to stop smoking.

Beezus has an assignment to interview a senior citizen about something they did as a child. The only old person the family knows is their neighbor, Mrs. Swink. Shy Beezus gladly accepts Ramona's offer to go along. Mrs. Swink tells the girls a little about her childhood and then, prompted by a question from Ramona, remembers about tin-can stilts, explaining their construction and use. Beezus has the material she needs for her assignment, and Ramona cannot wait to tell Howie about the stilts. He makes two pairs from empty coffee cans, and they spend several happy days clanking around the block singing, "Ninety-nine bottles of beer on the wall."

One Sunday in early December, the Sunday school superintendent begins plans for the Christmas Program. Henry Huggins will be Joseph and Beezus will be Mary. Ramona suggests that she be a sheep and is told that she will have to provide her own costume. With limited funds for such things, and with Mother's tight schedule, there is little progress on a sheep suit for Ramona, but Davy and Howie have beautiful homemade sheep costumes.

Then, suddenly, Father finds a job. He will be a checker in a supermarket, with a chance for advancement. The family is happy again, although Beezus just goes around looking serene, practicing for her Mary role. On the night of the Christmas program, Ramona is ashamed of the make-shift sheep suit her mother has concocted. She hides in a corner of the Sunday school room and even Beezus, looking serene in her Mary costume, cannot persuade her to come out.

Ramona has a change of heart and wishes she could join in the preparations, but she said she would not be in the program, so she cannot back down now. She silently prays that God will find a way out of the mess she has made. Three older girls are putting on makeup, and Ramona tells them that she could be a sheep if she had a black nose. Their mascara does the trick, and Ramona happily takes her place with Howie and Davy, who want black noses, too. The program begins and the cast is transformed by the beauty of the lights, the music, and the story. Ramona is so happy that she cannot resist a joyful "Baa" and a wiggle of her tail.

♦ *Ramona and Her Father* was named a Newbery Honor Book in 1978 and a Boston Globe Horn Book Honor Book the same year. State awards include the Garden State Children's Award in 1980, the Land of Enchantment in 1981, the Nene in 1979, the Volunteer in 1980, the Texas Bluebonnet in 1981, and the Utah Children's Choice in 1980. *Ramona and Her Father* received the Young Reader's Choice Award in 1980 and was listed on the International Board on Books for Young People Honor list in 1980.

Ramona and Her Mother

(New York: Morrow, 1979)

Illustrated by Alan Tiegreen

The Quimbys are giving a New Year's Day brunch to celebrate Father's new job, and they have invited all the neighbors. Ramona has been given the task of watching Willa Jean, Howie's pesty little sister, while Beezus will help her mother serve the brunch. Ramona has wrapped up a large box of Kleenex as a gift for Willa Jean and explains that she has always thought it would be fun to pull one Kleenex at a time from the box until it is empty. Willa Jean races around among the guests throwing tissues in the air as they struggle to balance plates and cups. Ramona decides that Willa Jean is a spoiled pest and is horrified when she overhears a departing guest remark that the little girl reminds them of Ramona at that age. Another guest says that Beezus is certainly her mother's girl, and Mother replies that she could not get along without her. Ramona is filled with jealousy.

One rainy Saturday, Mother and the girls are all sewing on different projects. Ramona has a temper tantrum when her project does not turn out right, but Beezus's is perfect. Ramona is sent to her room, and finds a brand new tube of toothpaste tempting her in the bathroom. She has always wanted to squirt all the toothpaste out of a tube, and so she does, designing intricate patterns in the sink. Even when she is discovered and scolded, she is happy because she has done something she has always wanted to do.

After-school care has been arranged at the Kemp's, where Howie's grandmother baby-sits for her two grandchildren and Ramona. Howie and Ramona get along just fine, but Willa Jean, Mrs. Kemp's favorite, is a pampered nuisance. There is a bad day when Howie and Ramona, playing with a boat in the basement sink, spill a bottle of laundry bluing and turn blue themselves. Mrs. Kemp blames Ramona for all the trouble, and Ramona feels out of place and unhappy as she waits for her family. The situation worsens when the Quimby's finally get home, only to find that someone forgot to turn on the Crock-Pot in the morning, so now there is only cold, uncooked meat and vegetables.

Everyone is tired and hungry and cross. Mother and Father both blame each other for forgetting to plug in the appliance, and over a pancake supper their bickering turns into a real argument. The girls are shocked and upset. They go to bed quietly, without being told, then whisper together, worrying about the possibility of divorce. The next morning they are surprised to find everything back to normal and, when Ramona angrily scolds her parents for arguing, they explain that parents are sometimes short-tempered and cross, and they certainly are not perfect. Ramona haughtily tells them not to do that again, and they agree.

Beezus, whom Mother has said is in "a difficult stage," no longer wants her mother to cut her hair; she wants it professionally styled and cut. Citing the cost, Mother refuses and a silent war ensues between them. Finally Beezus tells the family about Robert's School of Hair Design, where it costs less to have hair done by students. She offers to pay for it herself and Mother agrees to take her across town to the school. They have a harrowing trip, with Ramona getting carsick and Mother getting lost. While Ramona and Mother wait for Beezus, Robert himself offers to cut Ramona's hair at half price. Ramona is thrilled with the results, and even Mother is pleased. Unfortunately, poor Beezus has been given a hairdo for a middle-aged woman. She is distraught, but Mother assures her it will all wash out.

Ramona can tell her parents are having serious discussions again, and she suspects they are about her. Her mother buys her a new pair of flannel pajamas that Ramona likes so much she does not want to take them off in the morning. She wears them to school under her clothes but soon is hot and uncomfortable, and her teacher realizes something is wrong. She promises not to tell anyone that Ramona has on pajamas and suggests that she take them off in the girl's bathroom and hide them in her desk. That evening Ramona realizes she forgot her pajamas at school and will have to hide her silliness from her family all weekend long. The family is cleaning the house the next morning when Mrs. Rudge phones and talks to Mother a long time. Ramona is certain she has told about the pajamas and she flies into a frenzy, saying that her teacher had promised not to tell about the pajamas.

Ramona declares that she will run away, but is disappointed when Mother offers to help her pack and even supplies a large suitcase. Mother fills the suitcase, but when she is finished it is too heavy for Ramona to pick up. She admits she tricked her because she just could not get along without Ramona. They hug and all is forgiven and explained. Ramona knows that she is still her mother's "little rabbit," and Mother reveals future plans. Daddy will quit his job at the market and go back to school to earn his college degree to get a better job. This means that Mother will have to continue to work full-time, and Ramona will have to continue to go to Howie's house after school. She will have to put up with Willa Jean and Mrs. Kemp, and they all will scrimp and pinch to save money.

♦ *Ramona and Her Mother* received the American Book Award for Children's Fiction in 1981, the Garden State Award for Younger Fiction in 1982, and the Surrey School Award in 1982.

Ramona Quimby, Age 8

(New York: Morrow, 1981)

Illustrated by Alan Tiegreen

School has started again, but this year things are quite different. Ramona will take a school bus to Cedarhurst Primary School for third grade because Glenwood has been changed to an intermediate school. Beezus will go to Rosemont Junior High, and Daddy will start classes in college and work part-time in the frozen-food warehouse of a supermarket chain. Only Mother will be going to the same place this fall when she continues to work in a doctor's office, and of course Ramona will still be going to the Kemp house after school and will still be expected to be nice to Howie's little sister, Willa Jean. Ramona fears that if she is not nice to Willa Jean, her mother will have to quit work to stay home with her, and then her father will not be able to stay in school because he will have to get a full-time job to make up for Mrs. Quimby's lost income. It is quite a responsibility and a worry for an eight-year-old.

Ramona enjoys riding on the school bus, but a boy encountered on the way teases Ramona. She calls him "Yard Ape" and is annoyed to find that he is in her class.

The after-school situation at the Kemp house becomes even worse for Ramona. She longs to curl up and read but Willa Jean will not leave her alone. Mrs. Kemp insists that Ramona entertain the child, and even Beezus cannot help because she is busy doing her homework. At last Ramona tells Willa Jean she has homework to do called "Sustained Silent Reading," so at least for a while, she is able to read quietly.

Ramona loves her teacher, Mrs. Whaley, and finds third grade very interesting. Then one day Ramona joins in the current fad of eating a hard-boiled egg for lunch. The eggshell must be broken by whacking it against the head, but Ramona finds, to her horror, that her mother has forgotten to boil her egg. Sent to the office to have the raw egg cleaned out of her hair, she overhears her teacher talking to the secretary and mistakenly thinks Mrs. Whaley has called her a nuisance. She is devastated and only a little mollified when Yard Ape tells her she is a good kid and calls her an "egghead."

Both girls complain loudly when they realize that the dinner they thought was pot roast is really tongue. Their father is irritated and tells them that they will prepare dinner the next day. They actually enjoy being creative with the food that is available, and the resulting dinner is nutritious and tasty, although the mess in the kitchen is extensive.

At school Ramona tries very hard not to be a nuisance to Mrs. Whaley, but school has turned into something she dreads each day. She feels sick one day, but does not want to bother her teacher, and the worse possible thing happens—she throws up on the classroom floor. She is taken to the office, and later Mother comes to take her home and put her to bed.

Mother stays home from work to care for Ramona for a few days, but Father comes home with the bad news that the car needs expensive repairs. Mrs. Whaley sends a book home for Ramona to read and report on by "selling" it to her class. She also receives get-well notes from each classmate, and she likes the one from Yard Ape the best.

When Ramona recovers, she has to decide how she will "sell" her book. The book, a story about a cat, is not one that she has especially enjoyed. Her father suggests doing a commercial similar to the ones she watches on television. She creates a skit complete with three masks and enlists the help of two friends. The resulting performance sends the class and Mrs. Whaley into gales of laughter and is a tremendous hit. Mrs.

Whaley praises Ramona's creativity, and Ramona is pleased to learn that she had misunderstood her teacher, and that Mrs. Whaley does not think that she is a nuisance and truly likes her.

It is a rainy Sunday, and everyone in the Quimby household is getting on everyone else's nerves. Beezus frets because her mother will not let her go to a slumber party, Ramona does not want to clean up her room, Daddy is having trouble with his homework, and Mother is anxiously trying to stretch their money to pay bills. Suddenly, just when things look gloomiest, Daddy declares that, in spite of the cost, they will all go to the Whopperburger for dinner. On the way, they decide that during dinner they will all be happy and kind to each other because they have been so grumpy lately. While they are waiting for a table, an elderly man comes up and begins to talk to a surprised and embarrassed Ramona. He is later seated at a table near theirs, and to her surprise, he winks at her. They enjoy their dinner and remember not to say anything negative or cross. When they get ready to leave, the waitress tells them that their bill has been paid by the elderly man who just left. She says he did it because they seemed to be such a nice family and he missed his own children. The surprised Quimbys drive home and decide that he was right. They are a very nice family—most of the time. Ramona also decides to make things easier for her very nice family by trying harder to get along with Willa Jean and with Mrs. Whaley.

♦ *Ramona Quimby, Age 8* was named a Newbery Honor Book in 1982, was given the Garden State Award for Younger Fiction in 1984, the Michigan Young Reader's Award in 1984; and the Sunshine State Young Readers Award in 1984.

Ramona Forever

(New York: Morrow, 1984)

Illustrated by Alan Tiegreen

Getting along at the Kemp house after school is not easy for Ramona. Howie's rich Uncle Hobart is coming home after living and working in the oil fields of Saudi Arabia, and Ramona discovers that both Aunt Bea and Mother remember him as a cute boy who went to high school with them. After days of anticipation, the rich uncle finally arrives and brings gifts for Willa Jean and Howie. Ramona is disappointed to find that he is just an ordinary, young man with whiskers and jeans who is a big tease. Uncle Hobart brings Howie a unicycle, and while they practice with it outside, Willa Jean tries to play her new accordion inside. Howie's grandmother puts Ramona in charge of Willa Jean and hurries outside to watch anxiously, for she is sure Howie will have an accident. Willa Jean becomes frustrated with her inability to make the accordion work, so she jumps on it, bursting the bellow. Ramona is horrified, but when Mrs. Kemp sees what has happened, she blames Ramona for not stopping Willa Jean. Ramona is banished to a chair, and when Howie comes in crying with a bloodied knee, his grandmother embarrasses Ramona in front of everyone. Ramona realizes with shock that Mrs. Kemp does not like her, and she decides that she will never go back to the Kemp's again.

That evening at dinner Ramona makes the announcement of her decision not to return to Mrs. Kemp's house. To her surprise, her sister, who usually visits a friend after school instead of going to the Kemp's, supports her. Beezus suggests that she baby-sit for Ramona at their own house after school. Her parents agree to try the arrangement for a week. Later Beezus admits to Ramona that she has not been going to her friend's because she has been teased about Father not having a real job. She also confides her shocking suspicion that Mother is going to have a baby. Ramona is disbelieving, unable to imagine why her parents would want a baby when they already have two girls.

The girls are uncommonly good as they begin the experimental week. Several quiet afternoons pass without mishap. Then Howie comes over with his two-wheeler bike so Ramona can learn to ride, but Beezus is reluctant to allow her to go outside to play. Ramona reacts angrily, accusing Beezus of being bossy and calling her "Pizza Face." She storms out of the house to play with Howie, but before the door closes she sees Beezus start to cry. Learning to ride Howie's bike is not as much fun because she is worried about Beezus, but she learns anyway, gaining confidence as she speeds down the street. An unlucky turn causes a spill, and Ramona has a badly bloodied knee and elbow. She limps into the house and calls to Beezus, but Beezus angrily refuses to help. Ramona realizes that she badly hurt her sister's feelings; Beezus is sensitive about her blotchy, adolescent complexion. The parents come home, but the girls say nothing of their problem, although they are nice to each other. Ramona longs to tell Beezus that she is sorry for hurting her feelings, but she is still bristling over being called a hateful little creep.

The next day Ramona and Beezus avoid one another until, after school, Beezus goes to the basement to find Picky-picky. She screams for Ramona when she discovers that the cat is in his bed, cold and lifeless. Because their father said they were not to upset their mother under any circumstances, the girls decide they will bury Picky-picky before their parents get home. Beezus digs a small grave in the backyard, and Ramona finds a box and lines it with doll blankets and a little pillow. After an appropriate ceremony with a prayer by Ramona, they fill in the grave and cover it with leaves because they have no flowers. Ramona feels particularly close to Beezus just then, so she sadly says that she is sorry for the trouble the day before, explaining the misunderstanding of her careless statement. Beezus is sorry, too, and they are both happy to make up.

While Beezus cares for her blistered hands, Ramona makes a marker for the grave from scrap lumber. When their parents arrive home, Beezus and Ramona tell them about the cat and how they handled the situation. Mother and Father are both impressed and proud of their daughters. They take that moment to confirm the girls' suspicions—there will be another Quimby baby in July. Though both the girls are pleased and excited at the news, deep down Ramona thinks that she would rather have another cat.

Plans for the future are in high gear at the Quimby house. Father will finish his degree in June and will have his teaching credentials. They all hope that soon after the baby arrives he will begin teaching art in an elementary school full-time and will be able to quit his job in the frozen-food locker. The family all anxiously watch the mail, hoping he will soon get a job offer from a local school district. In the meantime he is working double shifts and will also work as a checker in the supermarket. Mother will stop work when the baby comes, but is thinking about taking some evening courses at the university. In the midst of all this excitement, there are some mysterious phone conversations between Mother and Aunt Bea, and the girls suspect that their aunt has a new boyfriend.

Everyone refers to the baby as "It," but Mother finally calls a halt to that. There is much discussion about what to name the baby, and they finally settle on a temporary name, Algie. Worry mounts as Father receives no job offers, but finally one comes in from a tiny town in southeastern Oregon. No one had expected to have to move away, and Father decides to think it over for a few days.

Ramona begins to suspect that Aunt Bea is seeing the tease that she and Beezus dislike, Howie's Uncle Hobart. Her suspicions are confirmed when Mother tells them that the couple is to come for dinner. During the meal, Uncle Hobart breaks the news that he and Aunt Bea will marry in two weeks, after school is out. They will immediately move to Alaska, where he will work in the oil fields. To the girls' dismay, Aunt Bea says that they will marry at City Hall because there is no time to plan a wedding, and her sister's condition prevents her from taking a major part in the planning. Uncle Hobart says that he, with help from Beezus and Ramona, can put together a wedding in two weeks. Encouraged by their mother, the girls agree to help, but they have some serious reservations about Uncle Hobart's planning skills. In the midst of all the preparations, Father announces that he has given up trying to find a teaching job and will accept a position as the manager of a supermarket. Ramona understands his discouragement, but she is happy that the family will be able to stay in their house on Klickitat Street.

The following Saturday, Uncle Hobart, along with Beezus, Ramona, Howie, and Willa Jean, head for the shopping mall, where they order bridesmaid dresses for Beezus and Ramona. A three-way mirror fascinates Ramona, who dances in front of it and watches her reflection go on forever. They find a matching flower-girl gown for Willa Jean and an outfit for a ring bearer for a very unhappy and most reluctant Howie. They stop for ice cream cones, then march on to the florists, where they place orders for bouquets and boutonnieres.

Life begins to pick up speed; Grandpa Day arrives to give away the bride and Aunt Bea moves in with the Quimbys for the last week before the wedding. There are showers and parties, and the phone rings all the time. The Quimbys host the rehearsal dinner, and there are very tense moments when Aunt Bea discovers that Uncle Hobart forgot to order flowers for the church and the reception. Grandpa Day suggests that they ask the ladies in the neighborhood to contribute flowers from their gardens, and a few phone calls prove that his idea was excellent. Aunt Bea mentions that she has invited her entire third-grade class and a disgruntled Howie is sure that they will all laugh at him in his ring-bearer's outfit. Ramona worries that Algie will not wait to be born until the wedding is over.

The wedding day arrives with a flurry of last-minute tasks. The bathroom is a busy place given all the showers and shampoos that must be taken. Beezus and Ramona feel beautiful in their bridesmaid dresses and with their heads wreathed in tiny pink roses. Then Ramona discovers that she has outgrown the old white slippers she is to wear. At last, when everyone is ready, Grandpa Day arrives in a rented limousine with a real chauffeur, and the family leaves for the church. Ramona notices Aunt Bea's third-graders arriving all dressed in their best clothes. Just before the wedding begins, Ramona confesses to Beezus that her shoes are too tight, and Beezus says hers are, too. The girls quickly slip off their shoes and hide them; their long dresses cover their stocking feet as they make their way down the aisle to the front of the church.

The wedding ceremony goes on without a hitch until it is time for the ring to be taken from the pillow Howie is holding. To everyone's horror, it has been dropped and lost. After a few nervous seconds, Ramona spots the ring caught on the heel of the bride's shoe. She quickly puts down her nosegay and crawls to Aunt Bea's feet, where she retrieves the ring and returns it to the groom.

At the reception, Ramona receives many compliments for her quick action and for her pretty dress. She notices with satisfaction that Aunt Bea has taught her students how to behave properly at a wedding. Ramona suggests to Howie that they put the outgrown white slippers to good use by tying them to the back of the bride and groom's car. Howie and some of Aunt Bea's boys take care of that job in no time and Howie feels much better. After the reception, the Quimbys and Grandpa Day ride home in the limousine, and Ramona reflects on the perfect day.

Summer moves on, the visitors go home, friends and neighbors leave on vacations, and the Quimbys settle down to wait for Algie. At last the time comes, and Mother and Father leave for the hospital. Beezus and Ramona spend an anxious night alone, but when they hear that they have a new sister named Roberta and that Mother is fine, they are thrilled. The next day, when the girls and their father go back to the hospital, a hospital official tells Ramona that she is too young to be a visitor on the maternity floor. She must wait down in the lobby, where she fidgets unhappily.

A doctor, noticing her misfortune, tells her that she is suffering from "siblingitis" and he writes out a prescription for her to give to Father. Father reads it and hugs Ramona. Then he tells her that the doctor prescribed attention as a cure for her worry and anger. In a few days they all return to the hospital to bring home Mother and the baby. Ramona is eager to see this sister that Beezus has so glowingly described, but she finds the red-faced little person with wild brown hair to be a great disappointment. Mother says that Roberta looks exactly as Ramona did when she was born, and suddenly Ramona realizes how far she has come in her lifetime. Being a baby is hard work, she thinks, and she has made great progress in the business of growing up.

♦ *Ramona Forever* received a New York Times Notable Book award for 1984 and the Iowa Children's Choice Award the same year. It received a Parent's Choice for Literature award in 1984.

Ellen Tebbits

(New York: Morrow, 1951)

Illustrated by Louis Darling

Ellen is an only child whose best friend has just moved away, so she feels lonely as she hurries from her house on Tillamook Street to her dancing lesson. She is hurrying so that she can arrive and change her clothes before the arrival of the other girls in her class. She is terribly afraid someone will discover that she wears woolen underwear that has sleeves and buttons down the front and across the back. She is sure that she is the only girl in the entire school who has to wear such a thing.

At Mrs. Spofford's School of Dance she discovers that Austine Allen, the new girl from California, is there. Ellen tries to get her out of the dressing room and makes a sharp remark that hurts Austine's feelings. She feels terrible about hurting Austine, and during the lesson she tries to apologize when Mrs. Spofford is looking the other way.

Her troubles do not end there however, for during the lesson her underwear, carefully rolled around her waist, begins to slip down. The more she dances, the more it slips. Worse yet, Mrs. Spofford's son Otis arrives and makes a pest of himself by mimicking Ellen, who is desperately trying to keep up with the class while hitching up her underwear when no one is looking. Then Austine loudly complains about Otis and finally even bumps into him and knocks him down. Otis is banished from the class, and when the lesson ends, Ellen rushes to the janitor's closet to change. To her surprise she finds Austine already there and changing out of her woolen underwear. Linked by that embarrassing bond, the girls establish a friendship.

Ellen's third-grade teacher at the Rosemont School is Miss Joyce, the youngest and prettiest teacher in the school. Ellen loves her teacher in spite of the fact that she is never chosen to clean erasers at the end of the school day. She seizes the first opportunity to impress the teacher by bringing an example of a biennial when class is studying plants. There is a huge beet growing in a vacant lot near her house and she promises to bring it in the next day. Unfortunately, the following day is rainy, and Ellen arrives at school riding in the basket of Austine's older brother's bike, but she is rain-soaked, covered with mud and beet juice, and has a torn dress. Otis makes fun of her until Austine comes to her aid and makes him stop.

It takes quite some time for Ellen to clean up in the bathroom, even with Austine's help, but finally the girls return to the classroom, and Ellen places the huge beet on Miss Joyce's desk. Her plan is successful, for the teacher does choose her to clean erasers that day and even confides that the reason she has not been chosen before is that she always looked too neat and clean for the dirty job, but today she is pretty disheveled already.

Austine reads all the horse books she can find and dreams of riding, and Ellen mentions that she has ridden several times, but does not explain that her mounts were farm horses or side-show ponies. Her comment is misinterpreted by Austine, who is greatly impressed and tells everyone that Ellen is an experienced horsewoman. Ellen is ashamed that she has misled Austine, but is too embarrassed to clarify the matter. She goes on a picnic with the Allens, and Austine spots a stable with horses for rent. The girls are allowed to ride for half an hour, and Ellen's lack of skill is quickly apparent. She loses control of her horse, and he heads for the middle of a river. She is rescued by a passerby and then confesses to Austine, who assures her that she will keep the entire incident a secret, just as best friends are supposed to do.

It is almost time for school to begin in the fall, and Ellen has an idea. She wants the two best friends to have dresses just alike. Austine is excited about it, but her mother is not sure she can sew well enough to make a dress, yet she reluctantly agrees. Pattern and fabric are chosen, and Mrs. Tebbits, being a good seamstress, turns out a pretty dress with a sash around the waist for Ellen. Poor Austine's dress does not turn out very well; it does not even have a sash. To cover her disappointment, Austine unties Ellen's sash several times during the first morning at school. As the fourth-graders line up to go to lunch, Ellen's sash is untied again, and she hastily assumes that Austine is the culprit. She angrily turns and accidentally slaps Austine in the face. Austine supposes that she did it on purpose, and Ellen is ashamed and embarrassed.

As the fourth-graders get ready to perform the Pied Piper of Hamelin for the PTA, Austine and Ellen are not speaking to each other. Austine has a child's part in the play, but Ellen is only a substitute rat. On the night of the performance Ellen is called upon to replace a sick rat and she puts on the costume for the first time, only to discover that she can see very little out of the mask. During the play she stumbles through the rat dance, but then gets mixed up with the maypole dancers and creates havoc on stage to the delight of the audience, who believe that it is all part of the act. Before she takes off her mask, she overhears Austine telling a new friend that she was blamed for something she did not do: it was Otis who untied Ellen's sash in the lunch line, not Austine. Ellen now understands Austine's anger but does not know how to make up and be friends again.

For weeks the silent dispute between the girls continues. Then one day their teacher calls on the two of them to clean erasers together outside the building. After some very uncomfortable moments during which Ellen rips the sash on Austine's dress, they begin to tearfully make up. Explanations and apologies are made and Ellen's world looks brighter now that she has a best friend again.

Otis Spofford

(New York: Morrow, 1953)

Illustrated by Louis Darling

Otis wishes that he had a house with a yard like the other kids in his fourth-grade class instead of the apartment where he and his mother live. He wishes that his mother could stay at home and look after him instead of always teaching at the Spofford School of Dance, leaving the cross apartment manager to keep an eye on him. Otis likes school, for it is there that he can always stir up a little excitement, and neat and clean and perfect Ellen Tebbits is the best one of all to tease.

The fourth-grade is to put on a Mexican folk dance for the PTA, and Otis, who hates folk dancing, will be the front half of a bull that is to pretend to fight a toreador during the dance. His friend Stewy is the back half of the bull, and they decide to stir up a little excitement for the toreador. They begin by making a delayed entrance and then, instead of pretending to quickly give up and fall down as the toreador dances around them, they charge aggressively and, to the delight of the spectators, the bull wins the contest and is showered by paper flowers intended for the bullfighter. Otis is happy to find that he is in trouble with his teacher, the toreador, and with Stewy, the bull's back half, who had received several sound swats from the bullfighter's sword.

One Friday, Otis is especially eager to cause some excitement. He begins by chasing Ellen all the way to school. Then he tries to come up with ways to stir things up in his classroom. He decides to spit spitballs at strategic places around the room. Soon Mrs. Gitler issues a warning: if he does not stop, he will get his comeuppance. He is so curious about what she will do that he continues, and learns that his indiscretion has earned him the right to sit and send spitballs into a wastebasket the rest of the day. He soon grows bored and terribly thirsty, but his teacher only insists that he continue, much to the amusement of the rest of the class. Even during a fire drill he is not allowed to get a drink of water. As the afternoon drags on, he gives up and tells the teacher that he wants to quit. Mrs. Gitler tells him that she hopes he has learned his lesson, to get some water, then return to his seat. The water quenches his thirst, but he still has a bad taste in his mouth, so he searches in his pocket for something to chew. He comes up with a clove of raw garlic and tries a bite. Then he hastily exhales and the fumes cause an uproar among the nearby children. Otis is happily causing excitement again.

One day Mrs. Gitler brings two baby white rats to school and tells the class that they are going to try an experiment. One rat will be fed healthy food from the school cafeteria while the other one will have only white bread and soda pop. At the end of one week they will weigh both rats and see which one is fat and healthy. Otis feels sorry for Mutt, the underfed rat, and decides to feed him secretly to prove that soda pop is good enough to be served in the cafeteria. He brings vitamins and cheese to school but has a tough time finding a way to slip them into the cage until he hides in the coatroom at lunchtime and comes out when everyone has left. He can feed the rat, but he misses his own lunch. By the day of the weighing-in, Mutt is larger and stronger than the other rat and Mrs. Gitler says that someone has spoiled the experiment by feeding him. To Otis's surprise, Ellen bursts into tears and confesses that she has been feeding Mutt after school because she felt so sorry for him. When it comes time to give the rats to students who can care for them at home, Otis waves his hand wildly—he really wants Mutt as a pet, but Mutt is given to Ellen because she cares so much for him. Otis gives himself away by loudly declaring that it is not fair because he fed Mutt, too. Nonetheless, Ellen takes Mutt home with her, and Otis is dejected. Later that day, Ellen brings Mutt to Otis because her mother will not let her have a rat as a pet. Otis is delighted until the little boy in the next apartment accuses him of having a girlfriend.

Otis and his friend Stewy are taking a boring walk one day when they see the star of the high school football team, Hack Battleson, standing in his front yard instead of attending football practice. He tells the boys that he is late turning in an insect collection for a science class, and unless he has 30 bugs mounted and identified by the next morning, he will not be able to play in the big game on Saturday. Otis offers to collect the 30 bugs for him so that he can go to practice, and Hack gladly accepts. Stewy wants to collect the bugs, too, and instantly there is rivalry between the boys. Each starts off on his own to get the 30 bugs by six o'clock that evening. Otis works hard and even gets the little neighbor boy to help, but when he returns to Hack's house at six, he has only 29 insects in his collection. Stewy is there and has 30, but one is disqualified when Hack discovers that it is a spider. Then Otis has an idea and quickly finds a flea on Stewy's dog. Now he has beaten Stewy, although Stewy loudly claims that it was unfair because the flea must really have been his because it was on his dog.

The day of the first snowfall, Otis is exuberant, sure that he can manage to make something exciting happen. All the children long to be out of the classroom and playing in the snow. Otis is more and more discontented, especially when some of the boys tease him about wearing pink underwear. When Mrs. Gitler has to leave the classroom for a moment, Otis and the rest of the class take advantage of the situation by racing around the room, pretending to be cowboys and Indians. Otis throws himself into the part of a particularly fierce Indian who brandishes a pair of scissors and threatens to scalp Ellen. Then, in one horrifying moment, he chops off a huge hunk of her hair. He is as shocked as Ellen at what he has done. Matters are made worse when the principal and Mrs. Gitler enter the room and Otis is taken to the office, where he fears he will receive his comeuppance.

Early the next morning, a Saturday, Otis goes to Laurelwood Park to ice-skate. He is grateful that he has suffered little punishment other than a good talking-to from the principal for cutting Ellen's hair. However, he soon discovers that the kids at the ice pond are all avoiding him. Not even Stewy and George will talk to him, and Ellen and Austine actually tease him and push him down. Otis feels that he is the brunt of gossip and disapproval, so he decides to go home.

Ellen and Austine also leave, and on the way they grab his shoes and boots. The others laugh as Otis stumbles out of the park on his skates, chasing the girls who are running down the street with his belongings. He cannot keep up, but he does not believe that they will actually go home with his boots and shoes. Then he sees them catch a bus and wave to him from the window as it pulls away. He gets on the next bus, still wearing his ice skates, and then stumbles on aching feet toward his home. A little later Austine and Ellen show up and, in exchange for returning his shoes and boots, make him promise never to tease them again. He mumbles an apology and a promise, and his footwear is returned. Only then does he laughingly show them that he had his fingers crossed behind his back so that his promise would not count, and Ellen can expect that he will continue to stir up a little excitement.

THE CALIFORNIA BOOKS

Dear Mr. Henshaw

(New York: Morrow, 1983)

Illustrated by Paul O. Zelinsky

In second grade, Leigh Botts wrote to author Boyd Henshaw telling him his class's reaction to Henshaw's book *Ways to Amuse a Dog*. Their teacher had just read it aloud, and Leigh wrote, "We *licked* it." The next year Leigh writes again, this time to say that he has read the book himself, and he has a nice dog of his own now, named Bandit. In fourth grade he reports to Mr. Henshaw that he has written a book report on the book and asks for a handwritten response. The following year, when Leigh tells the author he got an A- on a book report on *Ways to Amuse a Dog*, Mr. Henshaw suggests that he read another book of his, *Moose on Toast*.

Leigh's sixth-grade letter to the author brings a change. He says that he has moved to a new town and includes a class assignment: a long list of questions he hopes Mr. Henshaw will answer "by Friday." A subsequent letter reveals that Mr. Henshaw's reply was less than satisfactory; it was too late and was full of funny but silly responses to the assigned questions. In addition, Henshaw has sent a list of questions for Leigh, but the boy declares that he will not answer them, "and you can't make me. You're not my teacher."

Leigh's mom finds the list of questions and insists that he answer them, so his next letter to Henshaw begins to clarify his situation. His mother has divorced his father, who is a cross-country hauler with his own tractor-trailer rig. He misses his father, who does not keep in touch, and his dog Bandit, who now keeps his father company in the truck. He spends a lot of time alone because his mother is studying to be a Licensed Vocational Nurse and also works for a caterer. He is lonely in his new town, Pacific Grove, California. He has no friends in his new school except the janitor, and to make matters even worse, someone is stealing all the catered goodies from his lunchbox.

At Mr. Henshaw's suggestion, Leigh begins a diary, and there he records his happiness when his dad sends him a jacket for Christmas. He tells of his frustration with "The Lunchbox Thief" and with his classroom assignment of writing a story for the Young Writers' Yearbook. He is lonely for his dad and worried when he doesn't call as promised, so Leigh finally calls his father. He gets the bad news that Bandit was lost during a snowstorm in the Sierra Nevadas, and he feels even worse when he hears a boy's voice telling his dad that he and his mom are ready now to go out for pizza. In his despair that night, he confides all that he learned to his mom. She understands his bitterness and helps him to realize the cause of the divorce at last. One day, still frustrated and lonely at school, he takes a walk among the famous Butterfly Trees, where he finds thousands of monarch butterflies clinging to the limbs of trees.

Things begin to look up for Leigh when he builds an alarm system for his lunchbox with parts purchased with the twenty dollars his father sent him. The first day he brings the device to school, no one breaks into the lunchbox in the morning, and Leigh cannot get his sandwich out of it without setting off the alarm. He triggers the device and it works as expected. Everyone is impressed, even the principal, and several kids ask him to help them get started on alarms for their lunchboxes. Leigh acquires a friend, too—a boy named Barry.

The deadline for the Young Writers' Yearbook assignment nears. At the very last minute Leigh writes a description of a trip he and his dad took in the rig and it earns an honorable mention in the contest. Leigh's teacher arranges for him to attend the winner's luncheon with a famous author, and his story appears in the Young Author's Yearbook. At the luncheon, the famous author Angela Badger tells Leigh that she liked his story because he did not try to imitate anyone. She calls him an author and says that she has met Boyd Henshaw, "a very nice young man with a wicked twinkle in his eye."

Dad shows up at Leigh's house one day in the tractor part of the rig. He has found Bandit and is bringing him to Leigh. He comes in for coffee with Mom and asks if there is any hope that things could work out between them. She says no; Leigh is sad but understands. He feels sorry for his dad and as he leaves. Leigh returns Bandit so his dad will have company on the long, lonely hauls.

♦ *Dear Mr. Henshaw* received the 1984 Newbery Award, and was included on the *School Library Journal*, the *New York Times*, and *Horn Book* honor lists. It received the Christopher Award in 1983 and the Commonwealth Silver Medal from the Commonwealth Club of California in 1984. The Hawaii Association of School Librarians and the Children and Youth Section of Hawaii Library Association gave it their honor book citation in 1988. Other honors include the Dorothy Canfield Fisher Award in 1985, FOCAL in 1987, the Garden State Award for Younger Fiction in 1986, the Parent's Choice Award for Literature in 1983, the Sequoyah Award in 1986, and the Massachusetts Award in 1986.

Strider

(New York: Morrow, 1991)
Illustrated by Paul O. Zelinsky

Two years have passed in Leigh's life and, while some changes have occurred, many things have stayed the same. His dad still forgets to call, still is late with support payment, and still drives his rig on long, cross-country hauls. Mom has her Vocational Nursing License now and works at a hospital on the night shift because it pays more than days. She is going to school to become a registered nurse. They still live in the same little cottage that Leigh calls a shack, and he wishes that they could live in a better house.

While cleaning under his bed, Leigh finds the diary he started two years earlier. He reads it and decides that things have changed for the better for him, so he will start writing again in his diary.

Leigh's grades have improved and he still has his good friend Barry. His mother got the television fixed, but Leigh does not find much of interest there. He earns money by mopping the floors twice a week at a catering business where his mom used to work. He still feels sad when his dad disappoints him, but he can handle it now.

One day Barry and Leigh head for the beach and find a medium-sized, tan-and-white dog. The pup has apparently been abandoned by its owner; it is cold, lonely, and frightened. After many attempts at friendship, Barry and Leigh managed to convince the sad-looking dog to follow them. They name the dog Strider. They decide to work out a joint-custody arrangement because Leigh is quite sure his landlady will not allow pets. Barry has a big fenced backyard, and his family will not care if Strider stays there during the day. They agree to also share Strider's expenses.

Strider and Leigh immediately form a strong attachment for each other; Leigh suspects it is because they are both abandoned. Mom identifies Strider as a "Queensland Heeler," a herding dog from Australia, probably an Australian Cattle Dog. She approves of the joint-custody arrangement but is concerned about what the landlady might say. They cannot afford a rent increase or another place to live. Mrs. Smerling, the landlady, sees Strider but makes no comment, and Leigh tries to avoid her as much as he can.

Barry goes to visit his real mother in Los Angeles for a month, so Leigh has the dog all to himself. Leigh often jogs with Strider along the beach, and he tries to avoid Mrs. Smerling. When Dad pays a surprise visit with Bandit, Leigh is proud to show off Strider.

Leigh buys a unusual, wildly patterned, multicolored shirt at the local thrift shop on the same day Geneva, a girl from school whom he has admired, greets him as she rides by on her bike. He is thrilled and astonished when she calls him by name. He is pleased with the shirt and plans to wear it on the first day of school, although Barry, home from Los Angeles, thinks it is dreadful.

Dad calls and invites Leigh to spend the day with him on the rig. They have a pretty good time, but Leigh realizes that his father is lonely and may have financial troubles.

The first day of school finally arrives, and with it the debut of Leigh's wild shirt. On the way to school he meets Kevin Knight, a kid who was new the previous year. Kevin declares that the shirt was once his and was given to the thrift shop by his mother, who did not like it. Kevin wants the shirt back and begins to chase Leigh. They race to school and tear around the schoolyard to the amazement and amusement of the kids. The chase turns into a daily jog, with both the boys improving their stamina and speed while gaining some notoriety among the other students. Even Geneva still remembers his name, and the track coach advises him to try out for cross-country and track.

The news from Dad is bad. Because of financial troubles he has lost his rig and is out of work. He shows up at Christmas, looking dejected and dusty, with a gift for Leigh. Later during Christmas vacation, Leigh comes down with the flu and is so sick that his mom calls his dad to come and stay with him while she is at work. Leigh finally recovers and returns to school, but he is reluctant to share Strider with Barry again. An argument ensues because Barry believes that Leigh is monopolizing time spent with the dog. Leigh sees himself as being nothing but a rotten kid with a bad attitude, and he soon sadly returns Strider to Barry.

Leigh is unhappy at home and at school, and he desperately misses Strider. He is pleased when Kevin, whose family is wealthy, invites him to his house after school one day. While visiting inside the sumptuous home, Leigh discovers that Kevin, for all his money, is not happy. He is another child of divorce and has been virtually abandoned by his parents. The boys decide that they will try out for the track team together.

Strider runs away from Barry's house and returns to Leigh, so Barry decides to give up his part of the joint-custody arrangement, although he will still watch the dog when Leigh is out for track. To end the uneasiness, Leigh confronts the landlady about keeping his dog and is relieved when she says it is okay but suggests that he build a fence for Strider. He enlists his dad's help in constructing the fence, and as they work he learns that his father now has a girlfriend and is happier.

Track season is in full swing and Leigh is improving steadily. He and Geneva are becoming close. They make a date to go to the Lover's Point Weed Pull together and have a good time as they work together on the community volunteer project.

Kevin, Geneva, and Leigh all qualify for the Rotary Invitational Track Meet. Leigh not only wins the meet, he tops his own personal best time. This feat is especially gratifying because his dad, along with the new girlfriend, and mom are there to see him win. As his diary ends, Leigh writes, "My dog and I have changed since last summer . . . I know that I'll just work to beat my own time until I get wherever it is I decide to go after. As in track, I'll probably win some and lose some."

♦ *Strider* received the Reading Magic Award in 1991.

The Mouse and the Motorcycle

(New York: Morrow, 1965)
Illustrated by Louis Darling

According to an article Cleary wrote for *Horn Book* magazine in 1975,[1] her venture into writing stories of fantasy began when her own son, Malcolm, had a difficult time learning to read. Remembering her own childhood problems, she regarded his predicament with compassion. The one thing he seemed to enjoy looking at in books was pictures of motorcycles. Unfortunately, there were few books about motorcycles written for insecure readers. Her daughter, who was a confident reader, offered the comment that she would like to read about a little animal, and Cleary tucked these thoughts away for future investigation.

The next element of this tale was added during a family trip to England, when Malcolm ran a fever while they were staying in a nearly empty, old hotel. There were no aspirin to be had in the middle of the night, but the next morning, along with an aspirin, she bought him some tiny toy cars and a tiny motorcycle. As he lay in bed, happily playing with the motorcycle, a story began to take shape in her mind. The last element appeared when they returned to California and a neighbor showed her a little mouse that had become trapped in a bucket, and that mouse was exactly the right size to ride a toy motorcycle.

Ralph is a young mouse who lives on the second floor of an old hotel somewhere in the Sierra Nevadas east of San Francisco. He and his mother and younger brothers and sisters live in the wall of a guest room, one of the two adjoining rooms rented by Mr. and Mrs. Gridley and their son Keith. They had not planned to stay at the Mountain View Inn, but traffic was so bad on the highway that they decided not to drive on to San Francisco, but to stop for the weekend.

Ralph watches them move in and is fascinated by Keith's collection of miniature cars and a tiny toy motorcycle. After the boy leaves to go to dinner with his parents, Ralph seizes the chance to try out the motorcycle left on the bedside table. Although it does not really run, Ralph is thrilled just to sit on it and coast and finds that it is just the right size for a mouse. Carried away with excitement, he loses control, and he and the motorcycle fall into a metal wastebasket.

Some time later he is discovered by Keith, who suspects that Ralph drove his motorcycle. The mouse confesses, and Keith not only rescues him but shows him how to make the motorcycle go by making a "Pb-pb-b-b-b" sound. The two become friends as Ralph tears around the room on the cycle. Keith agrees to let Ralph take it out for a spin in the hall during the night, as long as he promises to return it before morning so that the boy can play with it during the day. He even provides Ralph with a tiny crash helmet to wear while he is adventuring.

Through a series of untimely events, Ralph is unable to return the bike on time. Keith's mother spots a mouse streaking across the floor on a motorcycle but does not believe her eyes. Nevertheless she reports to the management that she has seen a mouse in the room. This causes the housekeeper to order a thorough cleaning for

Keith's room, and Ralph and the motorcycle are nearly sucked into the vacuum cleaner hose thrust under the bed. He escapes the vacuum by riding away from it under full power but speeds into a pile of dirty sheets and becomes trapped.

The sheets, with Ralph and the motorcycle still inside, are dropped into a bin in a closet to await laundering, and Ralph struggles to free himself. He chews his way to freedom but has to abandon the motorcycle. Although Keith is saddened by the loss of his favorite toy, he still offers to bring Ralph and his family bits of food because the mice must keep themselves well hidden for some time as a result of Mrs. Gridley's report to the management.

The next evening, Keith becomes ill with a fever, but his parents are unable to buy any aspirin for him until the next morning. During the night, Keith's condition worsens, and Ralph leaves the mousehole, determined to find an aspirin for his friend. While traveling silently from room to room searching under furniture and in luggage bags, he is discovered, trapped, and tossed out a window by a hotel guest. He lands in some ivy and scrambles through a first-floor window. In this room he finally finds an aspirin under a dresser.

After considerable effort, including a trip in Keith's toy ambulance, he is able to get the aspirin to the boy, who then falls into a restful sleep. Ralph has saved the day and is a hero in the eyes of his family and Keith. His happiness is complete the next morning when, in addition to bringing Keith breakfast on a tray, the hotel handyman returns the motorcycle, which he had found in the laundry room.

As the two friends discuss what will happen after Keith's family leaves the hotel, Keith asks Ralph to go home with him. When he realizes that he would have to live in a cage, Ralph says, "No thank you." Keith then gives Ralph the motorcycle to keep, saying that Ralph will be the subject of his summer-vacation report. They decide to hide the motorcycle under the television set in the lobby where the maid never dusts.

While writing this book, Cleary once again had in mind the child who is an insecure reader. She remembered her son's dilemma when trying to find books written at his limited reading level, yet not babyish and about a subject interesting to him. She knew he wanted to read about motorcycles, but library books on this subject were too difficult for him. She recalled those boys in Yakima who never found funny stories that they wanted to read, and she certainly never forgot her own discouraging years of childhood when she found so many children's books to be boring and unattractive.

♦ The Mouse and the Motorcycle received the William Allen White Award in 1968 and the Pacific Northwest Library Association's Young Readers Choice Award the same year. Other awards include the Nene in 1969, the Sue Hefley in 1973, the Surrey School Book of the Year in 1974, and the Great Stone Face in 1983.

Runaway Ralph

(New York: Morrow, 1970)

Illustrated by Louis Darling

Every night Ralph races his motorcycle around the empty lobby of the Mountain View Inn, but he longs for the freedom of the wide world outside. He has heard about the summer camp nearby and has seen campers and their families when they stay at the Inn. One very reluctant camper named Garf interests him. A sulky, unpleasant boy, Garf is unhappy about the prospect of several weeks at camp, because he is sure that no one will like him.

Ralph grows sulky and unpleasant himself when his mother and uncle demand that he settle down and return to the second-floor mousehole. They insist that he give motorcycle rides to all his little brothers, sisters, and cousins. Ralph is so disgusted with the situation that he is determined to run away from the Inn and to head for the Happy Acres Camp. The first hurdle he faces is simply getting his motorcycle down the concrete steps of the Inn, a task that is accomplished with no little amount of effort and pain.

Once on the road to the camp, Ralph is triumphant and filled with optimism for a future filled with boys and girls and peanut-butter-and-jelly sandwiches. His arrival at camp is disappointing as he encounters first a gentle but determined guard dog who refuses him entry, and then a vicious cat who uses him as an educational toy to train his kittens.

He is rescued from the cat by a boy he recognizes as Garf, the reluctant camper. As he had expected, Garf has not made any friends and is considered strange by the other children. He is allowed to keep Ralph in a cage in the craft shop, and he sneaks away to be with his mouse during the mealtime songfests. Ralph considers trying to make friends with the boy, but he is horrified by the bloodthirsty camp songs he sings.

Life seems safe and almost luxurious in the cage, but Ralph soon becomes lonely. He welcomes the company of a hamster named Chum who comes to live in the next cage, and watches uneasily as the wicked Catso pokes a hole in the screendoor and then works to enlarge it.

Catso eventually gains access to the craft shop, but instead of attacking Ralph, he makes off with a camper's wristwatch, which had been left on a shelf. The loss is soon discovered, and unhappy Garf is accused of the theft. Banished from the craft shop, Garf takes refuge near the clump of bamboo where Ralph hid his motorcycle just before his capture. It does not take long before the boy discovers Ralph's bike, and then Ralph realizes that he may be able to negotiate a deal, for he knows the location of the missing watch.

Before he can convince Garf that he can deliver the watch, his plans are interrupted by Catso, who returns to the craft shop and attacks Ralph's cage. Ralph is able to escape and hides until he can speak to Garf alone. Garf agrees to return the motorcycle and crash helmet if Ralph can move the watch to a place where it can be found without implicating the boy. The deed is accomplished, once again with considerable difficulty and with the aid of a gentle guard dog. Garf's name is cleared, Ralph and his beloved motorcycle are reunited, and Garf promises to return them to the Mountain View Inn when his family comes to take him home the next day.

In *Runaway Ralph*, Cleary has sympathetically approached the anguish of the child who is an outsider. With gentle humor she has made it clear that Ralph, for all his bravado and love of independence is, like everyone, often very dependent on the kindness of others. *Runaway Ralph* received the Nene Award in 1972 and the Charlie May Simon Award for 1972–73.

Ralph S. Mouse

(New York: Morrow, 1982)
Illustrated by Paul O. Zelinsky

Ralph has been pressed to the limit by his bothersome little relatives. Rough, tough field mice relatives have moved into the Mountain View Inn for the winter, and they are aggressive and defiant in their demands that Ralph share his motorcycle with them. Worst of all, his old friend Matt, the hotel handiman, has been blamed for all the "mouse mess" they leave in the lobby, and the hotel manager has threatened to fire him. Ralph sadly realizes that he will have to leave the Inn to maintain peace and save Matt's job.

He turns to his new friend Ryan for help, the son of the housekeeper at the Inn. Ryan agrees to take Ralph to school with him, but makes the mouse promise to stay safely tucked away, out of sight. Ryan is a fifth-grader in Miss K's classroom; he has no special friends, but he is interested in another boy in the class named Brad. Brad has a BMX bike for motocross racing and his father brings him to school in a tow truck. Brad is not very friendly to Ryan or anyone else in the class.

Ralph is delighted to see the long, smooth halls in the Irwin J. Sneed Elementary School; he cannot wait to try out his motorcycle on them when the school is closed for the night. During the day he is an interested spectator from Ryan's shirt pocket, but he is discovered by a sharp-eyed girl. Miss K seems pleased to have Ryan's pet mouse visit the class, and she suggests several projects the class might undertake to learn about mice. Not realizing that Ralph intends to live at the school, she suggests that Ryan bring him back on Friday when they will hold a mouse exhibit with Ralph as the guest of honor. Ryan is teamed with Brad to build a maze for Ralph so that they can test his intelligence.

The first disappointment comes when Ralph learns that Ryan plans to keep his motorcycle and crash helmet so he will be unable to have those late-night adventures in the halls as he had planned. Ryan says that he will give back the motorcycle after Ralph has run through the maze on Friday. Ralph is hurt and angry and refuses to stay in the boot where Ryan deposits him for the night. He enjoys exploring the school at night and is pleased to find provisions and a cozy nesting spot.

In preparation for Friday's exhibit, the students in Miss K's class work on creative writing projects, pictures, and reports, all based on mice. A reporter and photographer for the local newspaper will come to cover the event. Ryan and Brad argue about the construction of the maze because Brad wants to make it so difficult that Ralph will not be able to find his way. Brad leaves the project, and Ryan finishes it himself.

On Friday, Ralph is horrified when he is put on exhibit in an empty fishbowl. He turns his back on the class and refuses to look at anyone. The guests arrive and the program begins. The newspaper reporter rushes in briefly and only hears a portion of one report before she dashes out again without talking to the teacher or any of the children.

Ralph is to run the maze as the grand finale of the afternoon. He is stiff from his confinement in the fishbowl and confused by all the strange smells in the air, but he knows he is to try to sort out the smell of the peanut butter and follow it to the other end of the maze. Instead of trying to find his way through all those perplexing little passages, he merely leaps to the top of the open walls and scampers over them toward the bait. Ryan grabs him before he reaches the end, and the test is started again. Once more Ralph nimbly hops up and runs over the maze to the peanut butter, and this time he reaches his goal. Ryan stuffs him in his pocket and the exhibition is over.

Brad calls Ralph "Ralph D. Mouse" and says that D. stands for dumb. He and Ryan scuffle, but because Ryan is trying to protect his pocket where his mouse is hiding, he is knocked to the floor, and the motorcycle, which is in his parka pocket, is smashed. Ralph is left alone in the school for the weekend to mourn the loss of his beloved motorcycle. He realizes he is homesick for the Inn and even his pesty little relatives, but he does not think he can ever return now. He is angry with Ryan and decides he will hide from him on Monday.

The children in Miss K's class are excited and angry when they arrive at school on Monday morning. The reporter has misrepresented their mouse project in her newspaper article. She has written that the school is overrun with mice and that the Superintendent of Schools has promised an investigation. The students are horrified, and Miss K suggests they write letters to the editor pointing out the inaccuracies of the report. In the meantime, fearing exterminators and cats prowling the halls, Ralph decides he will have to escape from the school.

He is still angry at Ryan, but he needs transportation to get away from the school. He decides that because Brad seems to be the kind of boy who understands a love of speeding bikes and motorcycles, Ralph will take him into his confidence. Brad is shocked when Ralph climbs up on his shirt and begins to talk to him, but he listens carefully while the mouse berates him for breaking his motorcycle. Brad confides that he has been lonely and unhappy since his parents' divorce, when his mother left. Ralph suggests that he and Ryan would make a good pair because they are both lonely.

Brad takes Ralph's advice, and he and Ryan work out a way to return Ralph to the Mountain View Inn. When they get there, they present Ralph with a mouse-sized Laser XL7 sports car of his very own. Ralph is delighted to be home again, especially with such a magnificent form of speedy transportation. He finds that only a few of his cousins have remained in residence on the first floor of the Inn. By employing classroom control methods picked up from Miss K, he is able to organize them into a group willing to share and take turns as passengers in the car.

In an epilogue, we learn that Brad's father and Ryan's mother eventually get married and the new family lives in a house in town. The boys are happy with their new parents and, most of the time, are happy to be brothers. Ralph remains at the Inn, where he gives rides to his relatives, but he is the only mouse who ever sits in the driver's seat of the sports car.

BOOKS FOR YOUNG READERS

The Growing Up Feet

(New York: Morrow, 1987)
Illustrated by DyAnne DiSalvo-Ryan

When Mother tells Janet and Jimmy that they need new shoes, they are delighted. The trip to the shoe store is filled with happy anticipation, but that turns to sadness when the shoe salesman discovers that their feet have not grown enough to justify the purchase of shoes. So sad are the twins that Mother buys them new red boots instead, boots that will fit new over shoes when they are needed. In spite of the disappointing fact that there are no puddles outside, Jimmy wears his boots all day.

Janet saves hers to surprise Daddy and quickly puts them on when he comes home. They even wear the new boots to bed at night. The next day there are still no puddles outside to splash in, so Daddy makes puddles with the hose. The twins show off their growing-up feet and their growing-up boots to the postman, who is satisfyingly impressed.

Hullabaloo ABC

(Berkeley, CA: Parnassus Press, 1960)
Illustrated by Earl Thollander

This alphabet book is written in rhyme and follows the noisy adventures of a little boy and girl as they explore a farm. The sights, sounds, smells, and feelings are those that Beverly Cleary recalls from her own childhood on a farm in Yamhill, Oregon.

Janet's Thingamajigs

(New York: Morrow, 1987)
Illustrated by DyAnne DiSalvo-Ryan

Janet begins to collect thingamajigs: a stone, a feather, a little wheel. She wants to keep them all to herself, and Jimmy must not touch them! Each day she puts her things into a paper bag, secures the top with a rubber band, and then deposits them in her crib for safekeeping. Her collection grows daily, and soon her crib is nearly too crowded for sleeping. A happy solution results when two new, grown-up beds are delivered to their house. Mother says the children are now big enough for these new beds. They are thrilled with this milestone in growing up, and Janet decides she does not need those thingamajigs anymore.

Lucky Chuck

(New York: Morrow, 1984)
Illustrated by J. Winslow Higgenbottom

Chuck has his own motorcycle, and after school each day he pumps gas at a filling station to support the cost. He has all the proper safety gear and a license. He had to study the Motor Vehicle Code to pass the driver's test; nevertheless his mother worries about him when he goes out on the bike. Chuck starts out on a ride and, for a while, is careful to follow all the rules for good drivers. Then, carried away with speed and excitement, he forgets all he has learned and not only speeds but drives in a reckless manner. Chuck is followed by the Highway Patrol and, in attempting to slow down, skids and falls off his bike. He is lucky that he is not injured. The officer gives him a ticket for speeding and reckless driving, and he also lectures him on the dangers of carelessness on a motorcycle. Chuck is sore from his fall and knows he will have to pump lots of gas to pay for his ticket. Next time he will be a safe driver.

Petey's Bedtime Story

(New York: Morrow, 1993)

Illustrated by David Small

Petey is not like most toddlers. He likes to get ready to go to bed. His nightly routine includes a bath, books, and a chase around the house before settling down in bed for a last story. His sleepy father and tired mother begin the familiar tale of the night he was born, but Petey soon takes over as storyteller and creates a fantasy all his own. When the wild and woolly adventure is finally drawn to a hilarious conclusion, Mommy has fallen asleep on Petey's bed and Daddy is snoring in his chair. Petey, fortified with cookies, crawls in their big, grown-up bed and falls asleep.

The Real Hole

(New York: Morrow, 1960)

Illustrated by DyAnne DiSalvo-Ryan

The four-year-old twins Jimmy and Janet like different things. Janet likes to pretend, but Jimmy likes real things. He decides to dig a deep hole in the backyard but his toy shovel breaks. His father comes to the rescue with a small, but real trench-digger used by soldiers. Jimmy sets to work again and soon has a respectable hole, so deep he can stand in it up to his knees. Everyone wonders what he will do with his real hole, but Jimmy pays no attention to their suggestions.

Father is concerned that such a deep hole in the middle of the yard is dangerous, but Jimmy is horrified when he suggests that the hole may have to be filled in. Father solves the problem by buying a small spruce tree to plant in Jimmy's hole. Everyone in the family helps plant the new tree in Jimmy's real grown-up hole.

Two Dog Biscuits

(New York: Morrow, 1961)

Illustrated by Mary Stevens

(New York: Morrow, 1986)

Illustrated by DyAnne DiSalvo-Ryan

Jimmy and Janet are four-year-old twins. When a neighbor gives each of them a dog biscuit, they set out with their mother to find a dog worthy of the treats. Unfortunately, none of the dogs they meet are nice enough to deserve their gifts, so they decide to find a cat instead. In spite of Mother's warning that cats will not eat dog biscuits, the first cat they offer the biscuits to eagerly gobbles up the treats. The children are delighted and think it is quite a joke that Mother was wrong.

MORE BOOKS FOR MIDDLE-GRADE READERS

Emily's Runaway Imagination

(New York: Morrow, 1961)

Illustrated by Beth Krush and Joe Krush

A comparison of this book with part one of *A Girl from Yamhill* reveals it to be the most biographical of Cleary's work. Emily Bartlett is a Beverly Bunn who is still safe and secure in a town where everyone knows her—a little girl who is confident that all adults love children. The setting for the book is Pitchfork, Oregon, a thinly disguised Yamhill in the 1920s. The stories related in the chapters of the novel are variations of the memories recorded in her autobiography.

Emily loves to read, but she cannot be a bookworm like her cousin Muriel, who lives in Portland. There are few books in Yamhill, but Portland has a large public library. Muriel always writes to Emily about the good library books she reads. Mrs. Bartlett, a spunky woman, decides to take matters into her own hands. She writes a letter to the state librarian in which she requests that a library be established in Yamhill.

Emily goes to town to mail the important letter and to see her uncle, who is the postmaster and mayor. While at the post office, she meets Fong Quock, an elderly Chinese gentleman who is liked and admired by everyone in Yamhill. Emily absent-mindedly corrects him when he calls her dog "Plince," forgetting for a moment that the kindly old man cannot make the sound "Rrrr." Everyone in the post office laughs at her embarrassment, and she finds out just how small the town is when, within minutes it seems, everyone in town is teasing her, calling her dog "Plince."

Mama has heard from the state librarian and is energetically making plans to find a suitable place to house a library and obtain book donations from the townspeople. She plans an elegant luncheon for the Ladies' Civic Club, during which she hopes to introduce the subject of a library. Emily is given the task of picking up fallen apples in the front yard. They are rotten, but Emily knows that food must not be wasted, so she feeds them to the hogs. The hogs gobble up the apples, then break out of their pen and lurch crazily around the barnyard, disrupting the luncheon. The Bartletts and their guests are mystified by their behavior until they realize that the apples had fermented and the hogs were tipsy.

Cousin Muriel and her parents are driving their new automobile from Portland to visit the Bartletts. Muriel writes to Emily that she would love to ride a horse while they are on the farm. Emily is afraid that Muriel will be disappointed with their plow horses. They are not nearly as elegant as the Black Beauty Muriel talks about. She decides to bleach their white plow horse, hoping it will look like a snow-white steed. She works hard at the job but is disillusioned. Lady now only looks like a clean plow horse to Emily, but she is pleased to find that Muriel does indeed see the horse as a snow-white steed.

Grandpa has decided to keep up with the times and buy an automobile, the kind known as a "Tin Lizzie." Emily longs to go for a drive with him, but Mother does not trust his driving. At last she gives in and Emily is allowed to accompany him on a trip to the country to see one of his farms. The trip is exciting and highlighted by the sight of an airplane flying overhead. Emily can see the aviator, waves to him, and is thrilled when he waves back at her. On the way home, the auto develops problems and Grandfather thinks that if he stops, it will not start again. To avoid that possibility, Emily jumps off the moving car each time they must pass through a closed farmyard gate. She opens it for the auto to go through, then closes it and hops back onto the running board. After opening and closing gates all the way home, she is shaky-legged by the time they reach town.

The library is about to open at last, with 62 donated books, 75 books from the state library, and Mama as the librarian. Space has been found in an unused clubroom over the bank, and several bookcases have been donated. The grand-opening day will be marked with a "Silver Tea" to raise money for the library. Those attending the tea will leave donations of silver coins, either dimes or silver dollars. Although Mama is disappointed that only sixteen dollars are raised that day, she is encouraged by two heartwarming events: Fong Quock donated a tarnished silver dollar that he had obviously saved for a long time, and a boy walked from a village miles away to borrow some books for his family to read.

The night her sturdy cousin June sleeps at the Bartlett's, Emily decides it is fun to tell ghost stories and be scared. June, who has little imagination, does not scare easily, but both girls are really frightened when they hear loud noises from the barnyard and see a ghostly white figure with a pitchfork in its hand. It turns out to be Papa, with Mama's help, getting their big bull back into his pen, but Emily and June have enjoyed their scare.

Emily overhears some ladies chatting at her grandfather's store, discussing light, fluffy pie crust made with a pinch of baking powder. The next Sunday, Mother is too busy to prepare anything for the church potluck dinner, so Emily volunteers to make two custard pies. She secretly uses baking powder in the crust but, when the pies are baked, is dismayed to find that the crusts have risen to the tops instead of staying on the bottom where they belong. The pies are their only contribution to the supper, and Emily is embarrassed when no one seems to want to try them. The minister discovers that they taste very good, and Emily proudly announces that they are called "Upside Down Pies."

Hard times have come to Pitchfork, and there is little money to go around. The library is popular, however. In fact, Mama cannot keep the books on the shelves. The ladies of the town decide to give a "Hard-times party" to raise more money for the library. Tickets will be twenty-five cents and everyone is to wear costumes of old, ragged clothes. Emily is horrified at the idea of wearing old, ragged clothes to a party and refuses to wear anything but her party dress. Even when Mama sews patches on Papa's oldest overalls for him and makes a dress from a gunny sack for herself, Emily insists on dressing in her best dress, even though it is more than a year old. The dress is tighter than she remembers, and in fact, she can hardly get it on. Her party shoes are also too tight, so Mama says that she will loan her an old pair of high heels, although they turn out to be a bit too large.

The moment Emily gets to the party, she realizes her mistake and is embarrassed to be the only person there not in a funny "hard-times" costume. She refuses to take off her coat for most of the party, then only removes it at her parents insistence to march in the grand parade with her sturdy cousin June. To her surprise she wins second prize for wearing a dress she has outgrown before she has grown into her shoes. She will use her prize money of one dollar to buy her mother an egg beater and still have enough to buy a copy of *Black Beauty* for the library.

Emily is at her grandfather's store when she hears the news that Fong Quock is returning to China after spending most of his life in Pitchfork. Pete Ginty teases Emily, telling her that Fong Quock wants to trade a monkey wrench for a girl Emily's age to take back to China with him. At first, Emily does not believe him, but when she sees Fong Quock in her own barnyard talking to Papa with a monkey wrench in his hand, she convinces herself that Pete was correct. She explodes in anger at her Mother, whom she believes has accepted Fong's offer, but is happy to learn that he was only returning the wrench he had borrowed. He did have a piece of business with Mrs. Bartlett though—he is donating his house to the town to be used as a library. Emily is delighted with the prospect of having the library as their closest neighbor and impressed with the old man's generosity. She makes a valentine for him and delivers it to his door, then returns home feeling like a pretty lucky girl.

Mitch and Amy

(New York: Morrow, 1967)

Illustrated by George Porter

Like the fictional Janet and Jimmy, and Cleary's own offspring, Malcolm and Marianne, Mitch and Amy are twins. When the story opens, they are preparing to enter the fourth grade at the end of summer vacation, and Amy is eager to start. Mitch, however, dreads the return to a classroom that will once again highlight his trouble with reading and spelling. Though they are twins, they are very different. He is very good at athletics and mechanical things; she is imaginative and loves to read, but has problems with arithmetic. Both children take music lessons. Amy enjoys practicing the cello while Mitch struggles with the French horn. Mother insists that Mitch practice reading in skinny little baby books that he hates. Amy resolutely refuses to learn the multiplication tables.

They bicker and squabble to the despair of their parents, but they help each other, too.

Mitch is proud when he builds a skateboard out of a board and an old roller skate, but runs into trouble when he is bullied by Alan, an older boy whose father is a famous scientist. Alan seems to delight in picking on younger children. This time he smashes Mitch's skateboard and chases him down the street. Although Amy is having fun with a friend, she sympathetically turns her attention to Mitch when she learns what happened to him. Her mother had given her permission to use the mixer to make the pudding for lunch, but now Amy offers to let Mitch have the fun. He is pleased but ruins the pudding when he misreads the directions on the package.

Except for a heightened problem with Alan, school starts out well for Mitch. He does well in math and enjoys the multiplication tests given on a phonograph record. Amy panics when her class takes the same test, and she realizes to her dismay that she will have to learn those dreaded tables after all.

Although they squabble, the twins do occasionally help each other. When Amy and her friends decide to scrub the kitchen floor to fulfill a requirement for the Girl Scout Housekeeping Merit badge, they end up with an ocean of thick suds on the floor. Mitch comes to their rescue and helps clean up the mess. When Mitch is frustrated by a school assignment to build a model of a sawmill out of toothpicks, it is Amy who pitches in to get the job done. When Mitch must read a book for a book report, Amy finds a book that he can read and that he enjoys as well.

Mitch's problems with Alan come to a head when they get into a fight on the school playground. The battle is broken up before either of the boys lands a telling blow, and Mitch finally realizes that he can stand up to Alan. Further trouble develops when Alan steals some of the cupcakes Amy and a friend are taking to a scout meeting. A crowd gathers as the girls confront Alan, and Mitch hurries to help them. Suddenly,

Alan shouts that he will wreck the whole box of cupcakes, "the H-o-w-l box!" The children realize that Alan has a reading and spelling problem, and while the rest of the group teases and jeers, both Mitch and Amy realize and understand his embarrassment and are sympathetic.

Cleary has said that she based this story on the experiences of her own children, but the anguish of the child who is having trouble learning to read is similar to that she experienced. Her son did not find reading a pleasure either, and Cleary seems to keep the reluctant reader firmly in mind as she writes. Although this book was written almost 30 years ago, Mitch, with his reading troubles and his confrontation with a bully, is a very contemporary character.

Muggie Maggie

(New York: Morrow, 1990)
Illustrated by Kay Life

Maggie is in third grade, the grade where everyone learns to read and write cursive. However, Maggie has decided that such knowledge is unnecessary because she uses a computer to write, and she calmly defies all attempts to teach her these skills. At first her parents are patient and understanding of her desire for independence, but they become increasingly irritated by her stubbornness.

Finally, her understanding teacher, assisted by an amused and tolerant principal, hits upon a plan to give Maggie a reason for learning to read cursive. Mrs. Leeper appoints her message monitor, who carries handwritten notes to the office and to other teachers. Each responds (in cursive, of course), and Maggie cannot resist peeking at what they have to say. She cannot read them but she is able to recognize her own name in nearly all of them. With her curiosity peaked, it does not take long for Maggie to learn to write and decipher cursive all by herself.

Several sections of this book are actually written in cursive, so it will make perfect practice reading for those who have graduated from print. *Muggie Maggie* received the Garden State Award (Younger Fiction) in 1993.

Socks

(New York: Morrow, 1973)
Illustrated by Beatrice Darwin

George and Debbie have been hoping all morning to sell their boxful of seven-week-old kittens, but no one walking out of the supermarket seems seriously interested until a young couple stops to look them over. They select the children's favorite, a rambunctious kitten that the children call Socks because he has four white feet. Socks is purchased and taken home with the Brickers and is soon firmly part of the small, comfortable household. He is blissfully happy with all the love and attention the Brickers shower on him, and he shows them affection tempered with firmness about getting his own way.

This happy state of affairs comes to an abrupt halt when the Brickers bring home another pet, a rival for Socks. This new pet is hairless, red, and wrinkled, and he loudly demands attention both night and day. They name him Charles William, and he causes total upheaval in the usual routine, but Socks takes comfort in the leftover formula he is always given when the baby finishes eating. Unfortunately, all that formula and little exercise soon turn Socks into a fat cat. The Brickers notice and put him on a stringent diet, which only adds to his unhappiness.

Sock's life brightens briefly when an understanding baby-sitter comes to take care of Charles William one evening. She holds the cat and feeds him and admires him. It is just like the old days for Socks; he glories in his one night of attention. Things take a decided turn for the worse a few days later when Mr. Bricker's mother comes for a two-week visit. She takes an immediate dislike to Socks, who is then confined to the laundry room each night. Tension rises steadily in the little house, and then one night Socks escaped from the laundry and finds a new toy—Nana's wig. He has a great time playing with the hairy thing, but in the process it is almost destroyed. As a punishment for this misbehavior, Socks is banished from the house to the backyard and the garage.

Miserable and hungry, Socks takes to sitting on window ledges, peering in at the little family inside. One rainy night he finds a tough tomcat neighbor eating from his dish on the back porch, and Socks gets into a pitched battle with him. Socks loses and is cut, bleeding, and muddy when he howls at the door the next morning. The Brickers bring him inside, nurse him back to health, and return him to the status of an inside cat.

Charles William is fascinated by Socks. He coos at him and crawls after him. His first word is "Ticky," an attempt to say "kitty." His parents are enchanted but still hesitant to allow Socks to get close to their baby. One day Socks comes into the baby's room just at nap time. Charles William excitedly rocks his crib until it moves closer to Socks, but in the process blocks the door. While Mrs. Bricker tries to find a way to get to her son, Charles William and Socks have a wonderful time together. By the time she gets a ladder and crawls through the window, Socks and Charles William are curled up together in the crib, cozy friends at last.

♦ *Socks* received the Golden Archer Award in 1977 and the William Allen White Award in 1976.

BOOKS FOR OLDER READERS

Fifteen

(New York: Morrow, 1956)

Illustrated by Joe Krush and Beth Krush

Plain and ordinary Jane Purdy is quite aware that she is not as sophisticated and glamorous as her classmate Marcy Stokes, whom she admires, but she dreams of meeting a boy who is at least sixteen (so he would have a driver's license), tall, and handsome. She does meet a boy that meets her qualifications, but at a terrible moment. She is baby-sitting for a child who is notorious for her misbehavior, and in the midst of a crisis, a delivery boy walks in the house and saves the day. Jane is charmed, but he leaves before she can find out his name.

He telephones her at home that evening, and she learns that his name is Stan. She is delighted when he invites her to a movie and even more thrilled when, in spite of her misgivings, their first date is wonderful. Other dates follow, and soon Jane is known as Stan's girl and is feeling pretty special. Her dreams are dashed when Stan takes another girl to the first school dance, but he later tells her that the dance date was made before he met her and that he did not have a good time.

Pleased with herself, a newly confident Jane begins to take on the silly, pseudo-sophisticated airs of Marcy, even allowing another boy to kiss her for fifty cents. Stan does not call, and Jane thinks that he is disgusted with her behavior. She realizes her mistakes and vows to be herself, no matter what.

She learns that Stan has been hospitalized with appendicitis, so she buys a huge bouquet of flowers for him and decides to deliver them herself. She walks across town to the hospital, encountering Marcy with a gang of admirers along the way. She manages to keep her poise, even in the face of Marcy's taunting, but momentarily loses her confidence at the hospital when she learns that Stan has been discharged and is at home. Undaunted, she marches bravely to his house, intent on delivering the massive bouquet. From his younger sister and his mother, Jane learns that Stan has often spoken about her and that he likes her.

Stan soon recovers and invites Jane to the class cook-out. On the date he gives her his ID bracelet and Jane knows that she is his girl.

♦ *Fifteen* received the Dorothy Canfield Fisher Award in 1958.

Jean and Johnny

(New York: Morrow, 1959)

Illustrated by Joe Krush and Beth Krush

Fifteen-year-old Jean Jarrett is not part of the "in crowd" in high school, but she and her one friend, Elaine, enjoy dreaming of glamour and romance. Jean is plain, small, and wears glasses, so it is not a surprise when a tall, dark, and handsome older boy asks her to dance at a party that she is only watching from the sidelines. Jean and Elaine set out to discover all they can about the boy named Johnny, and they prove to be good sleuths. By arranging to be in school corridors as he passes by, they observe his activities and friends. Jean is hesitant and shy, but tries to be cute and friendly. In spite of warnings about Johnny from her older sister, who is in one of his classes, Jean thinks she has fallen in love.

Johnny thrills her by making a date, but then, after making her wait an hour, calls and tells her he cannot come after all. Disappointed but undaunted, Jean continues her pursuit of Johnny and finally asks him to the Girl's Association Dance. With her sister's help she buys a new, ready-made dress at a smart shop with money she has earned by sewing. An overheard conversation between two older women wakes Jean up to what her sister has been trying to tell her: that she has been chasing Johnny, and he really does not care for her at all. She decides to break the date for the dance but is discouraged by the fact that she has spent so much money on her new dress. Before she can take action, Johnny tells her his grandmother is ill and he cannot go with her after all.

Jean asks Homer, a former friend of Johnny's, to take her to the dance even though he is short, plain, and wears glasses. He is clearly happy to be asked, and on the night of the dance he even brings her a corsage. The evening is almost ruined when Jean sees Johnny at the dance with a glamorous older girl. Homer suggests that they leave and go to his house, where his parents are entertaining friends. Jean is happy to meet them and is interested in Homer's pet homing pigeons. She is delighted that he seems to really care for her. Back at home she talks the situation over with her sister and is content at last to enjoy being herself.

The Luckiest Girl

(New York: Morrow, 1958)

Shelley is facing the start of her junior year in high school and is determined that this year will be different. First, she will break up with Jack, even though her mother likes him so much. Next, she has high hopes that she will become her own person and stop allowing her mother to run her life. All these plans appear difficult, if not impossible, until a letter arrives from a family friend who lives in southern California, inviting Shelley to live with her family and attend school there for a year. Although her mother dismisses the offer with a laugh, Shelley is thrilled to find that her father likes the idea. Over her mother's objections, plans are finalized and she is soon on her way.

Southern California is so different from Oregon in climate and atmosphere that it nearly overwhelms Shelley. She is delighted with the casual and relaxed Michie family, and finds the high school small and very friendly.

It is not long before she meets Philip, star of the basketball team and the boy of her dreams, and begins going steady with him. Both their grades suffer as a result, and when the first semester ends, he has lost his eligibility to be on the basketball team. In addition, his parents will not allow him to date at all until his grades have improved. Shelley is ashamed of her own grades and embarrassed about being the cause of Philip's problems. She is homesick now and wishes that she could return to her home and family.

As time passes, Shelley spends more time on her studies and with the Michies. She observes the conflicts that arise between Mrs. Michie and her daughter, who is several years younger than Shelley. Through those observations, she begins to understand her own conflicts with her mother in Oregon. Soon, friendship is renewed with Hartley, a studious boy she had dated only once when she first arrived in California. She finds that she has a wonderfully relaxed time when she is with him and that they have many interests in common. As the school year ends, Shelley reluctantly makes plans to return to Oregon. She is sad to leave Hartley but feels that she has gained in understanding and maturity.

The parallels between incidents reported in Cleary's autobiography *A Girl from Yamhill*, and Shelley's story are strong. Like Shelley, Beverly was shocked and angry when she overheard her mother talking to a friend on the telephone about her daughter's dates. Cleary reports repeated conflict with her own mother, and even dated a boy she grew tired of but of whom her mother totally approved. Beverly also received an invitation to attend school in southern California, (college rather than high school), and her mother spoke the same words Shelley's did when dismissing the invitation as ridiculous. In both cases it was the father in the family who insisted that his daughter be allowed the opportunity to experience life away from home.

Cleary's depiction of Shelley's gradual understanding of her mother and the sources of their conflicts are reflected in Cleary's own sympathetic treatment of the same subject in her autobiography.

Sister of the Bride

(New York: Morrow, 1963)

Illustrated by Beth Krush and Joe Krush

Barbara has spent most of her 16 years trying to catch up with her popular and beautiful older sister, Rosemary. Now Rosemary is away at college, having a grand time meeting new friends while Barbara is at home, struggling through chemistry, bickering with her younger brother, and longing for a boyfriend, but not tall and lanky Tootie Bodger, who clearly likes her.

An announcement by Barbara that she plans to be married at the end of the school year to a graduate student brings both chaos and (after Dad has been won over) happiness to the family. Barbara is thrilled with the romance and excitement of the wedding plans and throws herself wholeheartedly into the preparations.

Not everything is so sweet, however. Differing ideas about the wedding emerge from relatives, friends, and future in-laws. Rosemary, who is in the midst of term papers and exams, cannot give too much attention to the preparations but continues to cause concern with her intentions for stark simplicity. Mother is a junior high teacher and is busy trying to wind up the school year and placate everyone at home while at the same time keeping the wedding planning on schedule. Barbara has finally found a boy who seems interested in her as long as she continues to feed him cookies after school every day, but she finds that this only gives her brother fuel for increased teasing.

As the big day draws near, preparations reach a fever pitch. Wedding gifts arrive, gowns are being sewn, and showers are planned. Rosemary and Greg find an apartment that they will be able to have rent-free in return for acting as building managers. Barbara is shocked at the shabbiness of the building and the responsibilities her carefree sister is about to undertake. Rosemary has suddenly grown into a serious and practical woman, and Barbara is struck with the thought that Greg is lucky to be marrying her.

While the wedding is beautiful and Rosemary is blissfully happy, Barbara begins to realize that there is more to marriage than romantic dreams. Although loyal and steady Tootie Bodger begins to look more appealing, and her friend, the cookie-eater, proves to be truly interested in her, Barbara is not as eager to thoughtlessly rush into romance as she was only a few short months ago.

An interesting tie to Cleary's own life appears in the title of the term paper Rosemary must write. She struggles painfully with "Plato, Teacher and Theorist," the same paper that Cleary stretched to required length with carefully placed footnotes and wide margins.[2] The setting for the story is the Berkeley area where Cleary lived for many years, and Rosemary attends the University of California at Berkeley, Cleary's alma mater.

HER OWN STORY

A Girl from Yamhill: A Memoir

(New York: Morrow, 1988)

Cleary records in this autobiography the first 18 years of her life, and it is fascinating reading. Photos of her family, friends, and of Cleary as a child and as a young lady are charming and enlightening.

The real delight for an avid reader of Cleary's books is the recognition, on nearly every page, of real-life episodes that later became parts of one of her books. From the description of her mother who later was the model for Mrs. Bartlett in *Emily's Runaway Imagination*, Mrs. Latham in *The Luckiest Girl*, and Mrs. Tebbitts in *Ellen Tebbits*, to her vivid recollections of her anguish in first grade later reflected in Ramona, Mitch, and Emily, the book is overflowing with details that will send readers racing to her fiction books to check a chapter or a brief episode.

This is not fiction in any sense of the word, however. Cleary does not gloss over the financial problems that constantly weighed on her family nor the tensions that grew between mother and daughter. Those dismal elements are recounted honestly and with clarity. Her father's long period of unemployment and the haunting despair it brought to their lives is presented in a terse yet poignant voice.

She viewed these difficult childhood situations with sensitivity. Years later she was able to recall her feelings accurately, and, wonder of wonders, to communicate them so sympathetically that today's children immediately recognize these timeless emotions and know that they have been understood at last.

Like her fiction books for young people, this adult memoir of her early years leaves readers delighted that there is another in the series so we can find out what happens next.

My Own Two Feet: A Memoir

(New York: Morrow, 1995)

In this next segment of her autobiography, Cleary treats her readers to more glimpses of the stories behind her stories. Her adventures as a college girl, graduate student, career woman, young wife, and budding author are all recounted with her usual candor, clarity, and humor. Interwoven in all are snippets of material that can be easily recognized as the roots of episodes in later fiction works. The details of her first year at Chaffee Junior College in California clearly provided the material for *The Luckiest Girl*. Friends of Ramona will recognize her when Cleary describes a young patron of the Yakima Public Library who was applying for a library card. In response to the question "What does your father do?" she said, "He mows the lawn," just as Ramona responded to Miss Geever in *Beezus and Ramona*.

Cleary has frequently described in journal articles and interviews the circumstances and events in her life that have influenced her work, and these episodes are recounted here. There are also fresh insights, however, that serve to clarify her picture. The tremendous financial burden she carried all through her college days;

the conflict with her parents over her association with a young man named Clarence Cleary; the frustrations of a librarian on an army base during World War II; the early years of her marriage; and a cat named "Kitty" all are newly revealed parts of her life that will please her countless fans.

The book closes with the publication of *Henry Huggins* and a retelling of Cleary's happiness when she received her first royalty check. She joyously and accurately anticipated a long, productive, and rewarding writing career.

NOTES

1. Beverly Cleary, "Low Man in the Reading Circle, or, A Blackbird Takes Wing," *Horn Book* 45 (June, 1969): 287-93.

2. Beverly Cleary, "How Long Does It Take to Write a Book?" *Oklahoma Librarian* (July 1971): 14-17.

Settings for Books by Beverly Cleary

Chapter Three

PORTLAND, OREGON

The home of Ellen Tebbits, Otis Spofford, Henry Huggins, and Ramona Quimby.

The City and Its History

Portland is located in the northwestern corner of Oregon, where the Willamette River meets the Columbia River. It is the largest city in Oregon—485,000 people live there, and another million people live in nearby areas. The city is the county seat of Multnomah County, but Portland, with all its suburbs, covers a four-county area and stretches from the foothills of Mount Hood to the western plains of the Coastal Range. It is a transportation center with interstate highways, railroads, and a large airport, in addition to having the third largest port on the West Coast of the United States.

The site of the city was known as "The Clearing" to the Chinook Indians, who stopped there on their trading journeys. They had used much of the forest for firewood to fuel their campfires, and gradually cleared a one-acre area. In 1844 the original white settlers Amos Lovejoy and Francis Pettygrove called it "Stumptown" because of all the tree stumps that littered the ground. In spite of that, they decided to build a city there, and in 1845 they flipped a coin to determine the name of their city. Lovejoy wanted to name it Boston after his hometown, but Pettygrove liked Portland, after the city in Maine where he came from. Pettygrove won the toss and the city had its name.

Originally there was only a blacksmith shop, a tannery, and a sawmill in the town, but by 1850 there were churches, schools, and stores. The town grew steadily through the California and Oregon Gold Rush, the Civil War, and the coming of the railroad in 1883. By 1905, when Portland hosted the Lewis and Clark Centennial Exposition, it had become a mature city.

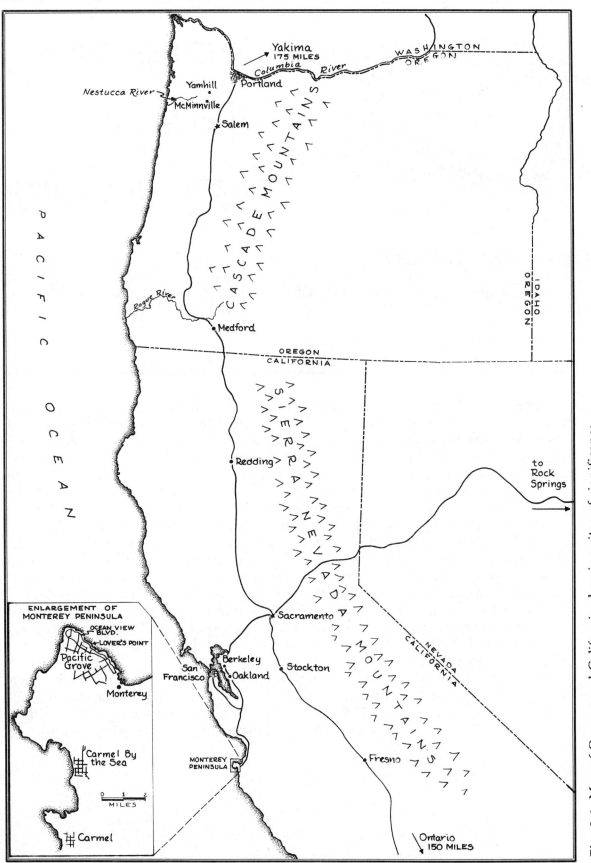

Fig. 3.1. Map of Oregon and California showing sites of significance.

Portland Today

Today, Portland is one of the country's leaders in the export of wheat and lumber products. There are many different kinds of industries, including factories for sportswear, such as Jantzen and Nike. Its beautiful scenery and pleasant climate have made it a favorite tourist attraction.

Home of the International Rose Test Gardens and known as "The City of Roses," Portland has a long history of concern for the environment, the arts, and historic preservation. Grand, old brick buildings can be found next to up-to-the-minute modern skyscrapers, art is in parks and playgrounds, and the water and air are clear and pure. There is a large system of parks and gardens—in many grow the city's symbol, the rose. The Portland Rose Festival is an important event that goes on for weeks, with parades (including the country's largest children's parade), exhibits, air shows, car racing, hot air balloon exhibitions, and of course, a rose show. In spite of its modern, big-city look, Portland has retained its small-town charm, with quality of life given top priority. It is no wonder that so many tourists flock there and that so many stay to make it their home.

Beverly Cleary's Portland

Although Beverly Cleary left Portland when she graduated from high school 60 years ago, she has always thought of it as her home town. When searching for a setting for her first book, *Henry Huggins*, she looked for an average neighborhood in a medium-sized city. The neighborhood in northeast Portland where she grew up became the setting for that book and for 14 other stories. The neighborhood has changed very little since the days when a little girl named Beverly Bunn played in Grant Park, ran up and down the Thirty-third Street hill, and tried to read every book in the children's department of the Rose City Branch Library. On the shady, tree-lined streets with tidy homes and well-kept gardens, children still ride their bikes, play games, and walk to Fernwood School just down the block.

Although Beverly was born in McMinnville, Oregon, she grew up in nearby Yamhill on a farm that had belonged to her pioneer ancestors. Those brave and courageous folks traveled across the United States more than 150 years ago. Her parents told her many stories about these pioneers and the hardships they overcame. She was often told to remember them when she faced hard times herself.

Her mother was a school teacher, and her father was a farmer. Beverly was born on April 12, 1916 and spent the first few years of her life growing and playing on the family farm in Yamhill. There were few storybooks in the house, even in the town, and Beverly loved to listen to stories. There was no television in those days. Luckily, her mother was a very good storyteller, so Beverly heard fairytales, family stories, and poems. When her mother ran out of stories to tell, she decided to start a town library. Beverly later told about this in her own book, *Emily's Runaway Imagination*, but she changed the name of the town from Yamhill to Pitchfork, Oregon. When little Beverly helped open the boxes of books for the new Yamhill library, she was happy to find that there were books truly written just for children, and she could not wait to start school so she could learn to read.

When Beverly was six years old, her family moved from Yamhill to Portland, Oregon. They rented a house near Thirty-seventh Street and Halsey Street, a neighborhood filled with children and just six blocks from the Fernwood Grammar School. Mr. Bunn went to work as a night watchman at a bank, and Beverly had a wonderful time making friends with the neighborhood children. At last, the day she had been longing for arrived: she began first grade at the Fernwood School.

Beverly did not learn to read as easily and quickly as she had hoped. She thought that her teacher did not like her, and she was ashamed of being in the lowest reading group. Very soon she found that she disliked school and hated trying to learn to read from books that were boring and unattractive. She changed from being a happy, friendly little girl to a shy, quiet one who was always afraid she would do something wrong at school. When she grew up, Beverly would remember those feelings and try to write books that children would enjoy reading.

Fig. 3.2. Although she never really lived on Klickitat Street herself, Beverly Cleary made it the home of her most famous book characters, Henry Huggins and Ramona Quimby.

When Beverly finished second grade, the Bunns moved to a house on Seventy-seventh Street near Fremont Street, and Beverly attended the Gregory Heights Grammar School. Although she learned to enjoy reading while a student there, it was not a happy year for the family. Beverly was pleased when her mother and father decided to rent a home on Hancock Street, just half a block from the Fernwood School where she had attended first and second grades. Some of her happiest childhood memories, which appear in her books, take place in this neighborhood. The area seems almost unchanged since she lived there more than 50 years ago.

Fig. 3.3. Beverly lived in this house on Hancock Street from the time she was nine years old until she was almost twelve.

Once again Beverly had many children to play with in a neighborhood where grown-ups were friendly and caring. It was nice to be near the Hollywood Theater and to find that not many things had changed at Fernwood since she left. She was happy to be close to the Rose City Branch Library because she had become a lover of books and reading. However, it was disappointing to find that there were few books about children like her friends and not many funny stories either, but she decided to try to read all the books in the children's section anyway.

Fig. 3.4. Fernwood Middle School. When Beverly attended, it was an elementary school. It became the model for Glenwood School, where Henry, Beezus, Ramona, and their friends attended. Henry was a patrol boy at this busy corner in *Ramona the Pest*. In *Ramona Quimby, Age 8*, Glenwood is a middle school like Fernwood is today.

Fig. 3.5. Across the street from Fernwood is a supermarket, the store under construction in *Ramona the Pest*. It was here, on a rainy day, that Ramona simply could not resist the

temptation to try out her new boots in the mud, and when she was hopelessly stuck, Henry gallantly rescued her. Next to this supermarket is the service station where Henry watched as Ribsy stole a lunch from a police car while the police officer shopped inside in the book *Henry and Ribsy*.

Fig. 3.6. Beverly spent many hours in this house located at Thirty-seventh Street and Knott Street, for it was the home of her best friend. Years later, in her books, Cleary moved this house to Klickitat Street, where it became the home of Henry Huggins.

Fig. 3.7. In 1928 Beverly's parents decided to sell the farm they had left in Yamhill. With the money from the sale, they bought their first home, a square white house on Northeast Thirty-seventh Street, just two blocks south of Klickitat Street. This house was Beverly's home until she left to attend college in California.

Fig. 3.8. Beaumont Middle School. It was the school Cleary had in mind when she wrote about Rosemont School, where Otis Spofford and Ellen Tebbits attended the fourth grade. It appears again as Rosemont Middle School, where Beezus and Henry attended in *Ramona Quimby, Age 8*.

Fig. 3.9. Directly across the street from the Beaumont (Rosemont) School is a unique building that certainly could be the place where Otis's mother ran the Spofford School of Dance, and where she and Otis lived in an apartment above a store.

Fig. 3.10. The elegant Hollywood Theater was brand new when Cleary enjoyed Lon Chaney and Douglas Fairbanks at the movies. In *Henry and the Paper Route*, the Huggins family went to the Hollywood Theater after Henry won the paper drive contest.

Fig. 3.11. The Hollywood YMCA. Henry went swimming here in *Henry Huggins* and *Henry and the Paper Route*. He first met Ribsy at a drug store near the Hollywood YMCA.

Fig. 3.12. Laurelhurst Park. Cleary changed the name of Laurelhurst Park to Laurelwood Park. It was while ice-skating on this pond in the park that Otis had his shoes and boots stolen by Ellen and her friend Austine.

Fig. 3.13. Laurelhurst School. In *Ramona Quimby, Age 8*, the name has been changed to Cedarhurst Primary School, and Ramona, Howie, and "Yard Ape" take a school bus here everyday.

Fig. 3.14. Westminster Presbyterian Church. The Quimbys attended this church. It was here that Ramona played the part of a sheep in the Sunday School Christmas program.

Fig. 3.15. Beverly Cleary graduated from the U.S. Grant Senior High School in 1934.

When Beverly was in seventh grade, she wrote a story for a class assignment. In her story, a girl talked to her favorite characters from books. Her teacher liked it so much that she told the class that Beverly should write books for children when she grew up. Beverly decided right then and there that she would do just that.

Beverly was in high school during a time called the Great Depression, a period when many people could not find jobs and money was very scarce. Her father was out of work for a long time, and the family had very little money to spend. Beverly remembered these hard times when she wrote about the Quimbys in *Ramona and Her Father.*

As high school graduation neared, the family realized that there would be no money to send Beverly to college, even though Mr. Bunn had at last found another job. She was a good student who worked hard, so it was especially disappointing to think she would not be able to continue her education. Then a relative who lived in southern California offered to give Beverly a place to live if she would like to attend the tuition-free Chaffee Junior College. Her grandfather helped by paying for her bus fare from Portland to California.

GOOD-BYE PORTLAND, HELLO CALIFORNIA

Beverly had decided that the next best thing to being an author was being a children's librarian, so when she graduated from Chaffee, she entered the University of California at Berkeley. After two years, she graduated from that school and went to the University of Washington at Seattle, where she learned to be a librarian.

Her first job was at a public library in Yakima, Washington, where she tried to help boys and girls find just the right books. Sadly, she found that, still, there were few funny books about the kind of average, everyday sorts of children she knew while growing up in Portland. She enjoyed telling stories and reading books to eager listeners, but when a boy asked for a book about "kids like us," she found that she had little to give him. She promised herself that one day she would write books for that boy.

In 1940 Beverly married Clarence Cleary, a young man she had met in college. The couple moved to Oakland, California, where, during World War II, Mrs. Cleary worked as a librarian in an army hospital.

Berkeley, California

The home of Mitch and Amy, and the Sister of the Bride.

After the war, Beverly and Clarence bought a home in Berkeley, California, a city in western California on the northeastern shore of San Francisco Bay. The city is the home of the University of California at Berkeley and several other schools and research institutions. Berkeley is a city of more than 100,000 people. There are some beautiful parks and gardens, a large marina where many charter fishing boats are docked, and several interesting museums. The city is also known for its many fine restaurants and bookstores. It is named for an Irish philosopher, George Berkeley, and during the 1960s and 1970s, students at the University of California campus led the national Vietnam War protest movement. Consequently, for some Americans, Berkeley became a symbol of discord.

In her new home, Beverly found some typing paper left by the previous owners. She told her husband that if she only had some sharp pencils, she would write a book on this paper. The next day he brought home some pencils and a pencil sharpener, so she had no excuse to delay. Finally, she sat down and began to write, and *Henry Huggins* was the result. Thus began her career as America's favorite children's author. She wrote almost one book each year for the next 25 years, always keeping in mind those children who had not learned to love to read because they had not found a good, funny book about ordinary kids doing ordinary things. She hoped to write books that children would enjoy and that would inspire a love for reading.

In 1955 the Clearys became the parents of twins, Marianne and Malcolm. During the next several years, Mrs. Cleary wrote many stories featuring twins as the main characters. Among them were *Mitch and Amy* and the series of picture books about Janet and Jimmy. She also wrote four books about teenage girls and their friends, but the books that were the favorites of boys and girls both were the books about Henry, Beezus, Ramona, and the rest of the Portland gang.

The Monterey Peninsula, California

The home of Beverly Cleary and Leigh Botts.

Today the Clearys live in Carmel, California, a small village on the coast of California, about 100 miles south of San Francisco. Just over 4,200 people live here, and it has been the home of many famous writers and artists since it was founded in 1902. The area is known for beautiful scenery, and tourists like to visit its well-known golf courses, many unusual shops and galleries, and a famous Spanish mission that was built in 1770. To the east are the foothills of the Sierra Nevadas, the setting for the series of books about Ralph and his famous motorcycle.

Carmel is not far from Pacific Grove, the home of Leigh Botts in *Dear Mr. Henshaw* and *Strider*. Pacific Grove, with a population of 16,000, is famous for the butterfly trees that Leigh found so interesting. These are pine trees that are covered with

Monarch butterflies from late October to March. Each year, the butterflies migrate to Pacific Grove from as far away as Canada and South America.

Mrs. Cleary seems to be able to write nearly any kind of story that children enjoy reading. She has written animal stories such as *Socks*, and fantasies such as *The Mouse and the Motorcycle*, *Runaway Ralph*, and *Ralph S. Mouse*. She won the Newbery Award for her book *Dear Mr. Henshaw*, which tells of a boy who is confused and unhappy when his mom and dad get a divorce.

Mrs. Cleary is still interested in providing children with good books to read. Recently she gave a brand new bookmobile to the county library system so that good books would be available to children who live far from a library.

HENRY, RAMONA, AND RIBSY ON DISPLAY IN THEIR HOMETOWN

Since 1992, plans had been in the making to honor Beverly Cleary in her Portland neighborhood. A group of teachers, librarians, booksellers, and neighbors got together and decided that it would be a great idea to create statues of Henry, Ramona, and Ribsy. What better place to display them than in Grant Park, in the heart of Henry's and Ramona's neighborhood? It was here that Henry searched for nightcrawlers in *Henry Huggins*, the first book about the children who live on and near Klickitat Street. Mrs. Cleary lived just a few blocks away when she was a little girl, and she often played where the statues will be placed.

The group of people interested in commemorating Mrs. Cleary and her storybook characters call themselves "The Friends of Henry and Ramona." They decided to raise funds to create a permanent monument in the park: three statues set next to a wading pool and a fountain. In the spring of 1993, they sponsored a play called *Ramona Quimby* and sold tickets to raise money for the project. They made a map showing many of the places mentioned in Mrs. Cleary's books and sold copies of the map to raise money. They sold T-shirts and bookbags with pictures of Henry and Ramona on them.

Children from all over the United States who love the stories set in Portland began collecting money for the monument. They developed projects such as collecting old cans and redeeming them to get the refunds, as well as holding schoolwide read-a-thons. They sent the money they collected to the "Friends." Major donations were received from business, industry, and government agencies, and the proceeds from the sales of T-shirts were substantial. Even so, it took five years to raise enough money for the statues, a fountain, granite benches, and a new wading pool.

Artist Lee Hunt created the three statues. Clay figures were shaped over forms; then the figures were dressed in clothes of the type worn by Henry and Ramona. Henry carries his baseball, and Ramona is wearing her rain boots. Molds were then made and the figures were cast in bronze. The resulting sculptures are very detailed and lifelike. Around the entire pool and fountain area are paving stones featuring book titles and quotes from the books.

The dedication of the Beverly Cleary Sculpture Garden for Children was held on October 13, 1995. About 500 Cleary fans attended and heard the author give a talk about growing up in Portland. Some of the children in the audience were second-generation Cleary readers, having been encouraged by their parents who enjoyed reading Cleary books when they were children.

Chapter Four

Extended Activities

PROJECTS REQUIRING ADULT GUIDANCE

Reader's Theater

Reader's Theater offers an opportunity for children to share a book they have enjoyed, and it suggests the possibility of enticing others to read the book. It may help students realize that literature can be even more enjoyable when extended to activities that carry on the excitement and pleasure of the book, even after the last page has been turned.

During a Reader's Theater performance, students read their parts instead of memorizing them completely. It is a fun way to bring literature to life. Selected passages are read orally, with students assuming the roles of the characters in the book and a narrator introducing the action and carrying along the narrative where needed. The key here is simplicity; no props or scenery are needed; no costumes need be devised. The emphasis is on good oral interpretation and expression to create the illusion of drama.

Reader's Theater Production Hints

1. This is theater not of action, but of the mind.

2. Facial expression and hand movements are used while other, more physical activity is merely suggested.

3. The script is always in the audience's sight; the actors may refer to it at any time.

4. Actors may stand, sit on stools, and use lecterns if they wish.

5. Costumes, props, and scenery are not required but may enhance the performance, if appropriate.

6. Sound effects or music may enhance the performance, if appropriate.

7. Spot lighting or special lighting might be helpful.

8. The narrator is used to establish the situation and to link segments together.

9. When actors are not in a scene, they may lower their heads, turn their heads away from the audience, or do something else indicative of being "offstage."

10. Actors should know their lines well enough to keep their places while glancing from their scripts to the other actors and the audience. They should be able to read their lines smoothly and with expression.

Begin by having students select several favorite passages from books by Beverly Cleary. Have them decide which of these has the largest amount of dialogue. Students may write their own scripts using as much of the original dialogue as possible, or scripts may be prepared by the teacher. Cleary's books are often episodic, with each chapter a complete story within itself, so they lend themselves readily to Reader's Theater. There is minimum description in her books, and this also is helpful when designing a script.

Prepare the scripts by writing the names of the readers next to the lines they are to speak. Then place the scripts in folders and attach them to the folder by stapling them at the top and bottom of the left edge of the pages. Students may wish to highlight their lines. Most students find it easier to read if they are seated; simple folding chairs will do. An introduction, to be delivered by the narrator, sets the stage by relating what has happened in the story up to the point where the performance begins. Readers may introduce themselves and the characters they are playing.

Because students will be reading the passages aloud and not memorizing them, they may believe that rehearsal is not necessary. They should understand that the more they practice reading clearly and with expression, the more they will be understood and the more they will contribute to the performance. If they can glance up at the audience and other actors occasionally as they speak, it will enhance the performance for the audience. To avoid having students staring down into their scripts, mumbling their lines with their heads bowed, choose a "focus": a person to whom the students will address their lines. This can be a spot out in the audience where they can imagine a particular person is listening, or they can turn to the student reading the part of the character they are addressing. Whichever option is chosen, all the readers should use this focus.

Following are suggestions for passages from Beverly Cleary's books that lend themselves to Reader's Theater presentations. A narrator's introduction and notes accompany each selection.

Henry Writes a Letter from *Henry and the Clubhouse*

CAST OF CHARACTERS:

Narrator	Beezus
Henry	Mrs. Quimby
Ramona	Sheriff Bud

Narrator:

In this book, Henry is busy with his paper route and is building a clubhouse with his friends. However, Ramona has become the trial and tribulation of his life. She finds ways to pester him when he is trying to deliver newspapers, and one horrible day she even locks him in his own clubhouse. He desperately tries to find a way to keep Ramona from bothering him, especially when he is tending to business. He considers writing a letter to the lady in the newspaper who gives free advice to people or disguising himself as Santa Claus and telling Ramona to stop pestering him—or else no Christmas presents for her! When Beezus talks about Ramona's hero worship of the host of a local television cartoon show named *Sheriff Bud*, Henry has a great idea: he will write a letter to the Sheriff and ask for his help. He has seen Sheriff Bud waving around handfuls of letters, wishing people happy birthday, pretending he can see people watching him on television and giving them messages that Henry had always thought were really silly. He is doubtful that the Sheriff would actually use his letter, but still he hopes it will happen.

(Note: The student playing the part of Henry might read the first two lines of the letter, and Sheriff Bud might read the last two.)

Narrator:

Two days later, Henry stops in to play a game of checkers just about the time the *Sheriff Bud* program is starting. Ramona is already seated in front of the television, just as he knew she would be, and Sheriff Bud is talking to his audience in television land.

(Note: Students may create their own lines based upon the dialogue that takes place in the Quimby living room, combining the two days of action into one.)

Narrator:

Will Ramona keep her promise to Sheriff Bud? Will Henry succeed in delivering his newspapers without having her pestering him? To find out the surprising answers to these questions, read *Henry and the Clubhouse* by Beverly Cleary.

Otis's Scientific Experiment from *Otis Spofford*

CAST OF CHARACTERS:

Narrator
Otis Spofford
Ellen Tebbits
Mrs. Gitler
Stewy
Patsy
George
Bucky

Narrator:

Otis Spofford likes to stir up excitement in his fourth-grade classroom, and he especially enjoys teasing Ellen Tebbits, who is always so neat and clean and perfect. One day Mrs. Gitler, their teacher, surprises her class with two white rats in cages. The boys and girls eagerly question her.

(Note: Students may write their own parts based on the dialogue in which Mrs. Gitler explains the scientific experiment. End this section of the script with the naming of Mutt.)

Narrator:

Otis is really interested in the experiment, but not for any scientific reasons. He would love to be able to stir up a little excitement with those rats. Each day, he watches carefully as Pinky eats cafeteria food while Mutt only has white bread and soda pop. He begins to feel really sorry for poor Mutt, who looks tired and cross most of the time. At the end of a week, Pinky has doubled his weight but Mutt has hardly gained at all. Otis decides that it is time for action! If he can secretly feed Mutt good food, the rat might outgrow Pinky. Everyone would think it was white bread and soda pop that made him grow, and maybe the cafeteria would have to start serving soda pop! Otis brings cheese and vitamin tablets from home and hides in the classroom at lunchtime to feed Mutt. Unfortunately, in finding a way to make sure the rat is fed, Otis has to go hungry himself. By midweek, the change in Mutt is noticeable.

(Note: A script may be devised from the dialogue on the second and third days when several children, including Ellen and Tommy, discuss Mutt's condition.)

Narrator:

While Otis is happy for Mutt and excited that he might have found a way to force the lunchroom to serve soda pop, he is more and more nervous about getting caught. He spends a hungry and very uncomfortable Friday lunch hour hiding in the classroom cloakroom, but Mrs. Gitler comes back earlier than expected. The final day of the experiment arrives just as Otis's determination is about to run out. Now he feels like Mutt is his very own pet, and he wonders what will happen to his little friend when the experiment ends. Is it possible that he can think of a way to keep Mutt as his pet?

(Note: Scripting may begin at the point where Mrs. Gitler weighs the two mice. This segment might end after Otis admits that he fed Mutt.)

Narrator:

That neat, clean, and perfect Ellen Tebbits! Otis is pretty mad at her for taking his rat! He stomps off home and finds Bucky, a kindergarten boy who lives in the same apartment building, waiting for him on the front steps.

(Note: Script a short conversation between Otis and Bucky.)

Narrator:

Otis is still mad and wishing that he had Mutt. All of a sudden he sees Ellen Tebbits coming down the street carrying a small box.

(Note: Script the conversation between Ellen, Otis, and Bucky.)

Narrator:

Read about the further adventures of Ellen and Otis in their books *Ellen Tebbits* and *Otis Spofford* by Beverly Cleary.

Finding a Dog from the Diary of Leigh Botts in *Strider*

CAST OF CHARACTERS:

Narrator
The Diary
Leigh
Barry
Mom
Mr. President
Strider

(Note: Because this book is written in the form of a diary, it is possible for a reader to take the part of The Diary, reading most of the sections of the story that are not dialogue and thus weaving the scenes together naturally.)

Narrator:

Leigh Botts, whom some may have met in *Dear Mr. Henshaw*, lives with his mom in a tiny rented house (he calls it a shack). His dad is a trucker who owns a tractor-trailer, but he and Leigh's mom are divorced. Leigh is 14 and spends a lot of time alone because his mom works the night shift at a hospital. He has a good friend named Barry whose folks are also divorced, but Barry lives with his real dad and a new mom. One day after school, the two boys are hanging out, just walking along the beach in their hometown of Pacific Grove, California.

(Note: The script might begin with the second paragraph of the diary entry for the eighth of June, with The Diary reading many of the parts that are not spoken. The dog's whimpers can be sounded by the student playing the part of Strider rather than read by The Diary. Script dialogue to the last three paragraphs of the eighth of June entry.)

Narrator:

Barry and Leigh ask other people on the beach about the dog, but no one has seen him before. They go home, but then decide to return to the beach with food for Strider. They race back with hot dogs and water, afraid that the dog might be gone, but he is still there, and he gulps down the food and water.

(Note: The script might pick up with Strider's first tentative steps following the boys and continue through the end of the tenth of June entry.)

Narrator:

Will Leigh be able to keep Strider? Will he be able to work out a joint-custody arrangement with Barry? To find out the answers to these questions and to learn more about what happens, read *Strider* by Beverly Cleary. If you have not met Leigh before, you can find out about his life when he was younger, when he wrote letters to an author and kept a diary in a book titled *Dear Mr. Henshaw* by Beverly Cleary.

Cleary Kids Bulletin Boards

Happy Birthday Mrs. Cleary, April 12

Beverly Cleary's birthday is April 12. Students who especially like her books will enjoy seeing their favorite characters depicted bringing gifts to her. For example, Henry might bring her a fishbowl with several guppies, Leigh might bring a lunchbox alarm, and Ellen might bring a large beet. The characters and their gifts can be drawn and cut out by the students and placed on a bulletin board with a large birthday card centered under large cut-outs of the date and greeting.

Where Are We?

Display a large map of both Oregon and California. Surround the states with representations of Cleary's books. Attach a long piece of brightly colored yarn to each book name. Have students identify the setting of each of the books and then correctly attach the loose end of the yarn to the California or Oregon setting for that book.

The settings for particular Cleary books are as follows:

All "Ramona" and "Henry" series	Portland, Oregon
Ellen Tebbits and *Otis Spofford*	Portland, Oregon
Dear Mr. Henshaw and *Strider*	Pacific Grove, California
Emily's Runaway Imagination	Yamhill, Oregon (although the town is called Pitchford in the book)
Mitch and Amy	Berkeley, California
Sister of the Bride	Berkeley, California
The Luckiest Girl	Portland, Oregon and Southern California
The "Ralph the Mouse" series	Somewhere in the California Sierras

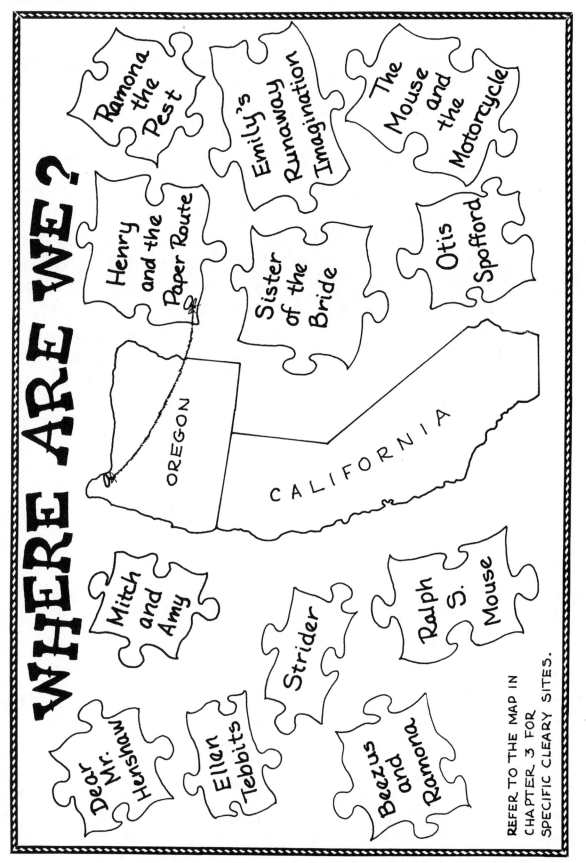

Who Is My Friend?

Have students work together to produce a list of significant characters in one of the Cleary series (Henry and/or Ramona, Leigh Botts, Ellen and Otis, or Ralph). Have students draw simple representations of each of the characters. Pin these character depictions on a bulletin board. Provide students with long pieces of string or yarn to link together characters who were friends. After all students have had a chance to participate, discuss what kinds of qualities they look for in friends. Which one of the characters would they like to have for a friend and why? When each student has had an opportunity to link at least one pair of friends, discuss which character seems to have the most connections to others. Compare the qualities of that character with the qualities of friends suggested by the class.

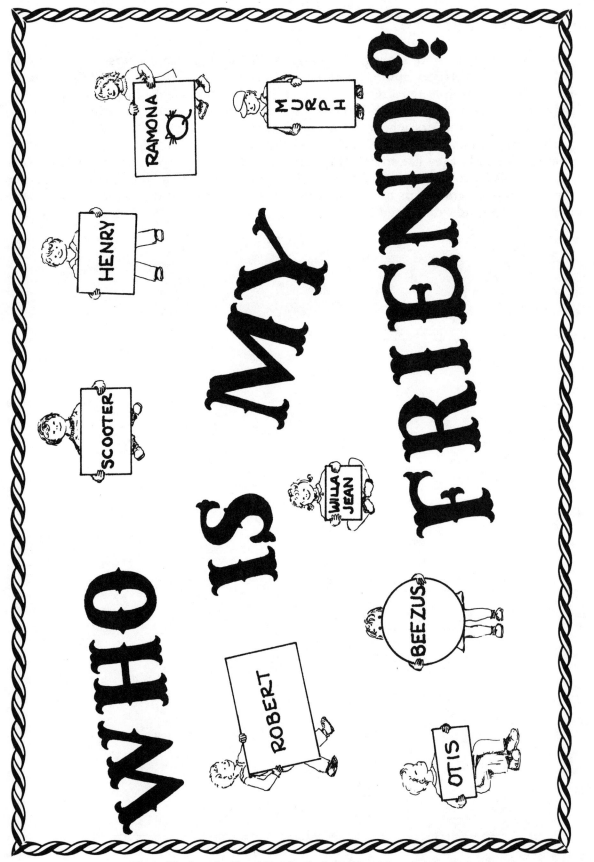

Who Might Say It?

Create and post a list of quotes that Cleary characters might say. Have students try to identify the character who would have said each quote. Have students write down the source of each quote and put their answers into a box. Later, display the correct answers next to the quote along with the names of all those who correctly named the source. Try the following quotes as starters:

"I used to hate my father, but now I sort of feel sorry for him." (Leigh Botts)

"Imagine, the nerve of them! Eating that cheap, disgusting food is certainly beneath my dignity. But tonight, when everyone is asleep, I'll show them!" (Picky-picky)

"Well, I've really done it this time! If I could only glue Ellen's hair back in place, I would do it in a second." (Otis Spofford)

"I'm so embarrassed, I don't know what to do. I'm, stuck up here, helpless on this horse, and I told everybody I knew how to ride." (Ellen Tebbits)

"I was told to sit in this chair to get a present and, no matter what happens, I will not leave this spot!" (Ramona Quimby)

"It's a dangerous mission, but I have to try. I will bravely go in search of the medicine. In spite of terrors like dogs, housekeepers, and vacuum cleaners, I will find it for my friend." (Ralph Mouse)

"I feel so guilty. I know it's wrong not to love her all the time, and I do most of the time. But once in a while she is such a nuisance with her silly imagination." (Beezus Quimby)

"Happiness is a boy to play with and anything good to eat." (Ribsy)

"I'm not really stubborn, but I just don't see any use in learning that silly way of writing, and I won't do it. I only wish I could read what's written on this note." (Maggie)

"Life used to be so perfect. Then along came that new pet. Now they pay no attention to me. In fact, I can't even live in the house anymore." (Socks)

"Sometimes life is tough. I don't want to read those babyish books anymore, and I don't want to be chased by that bully, Alan. Maybe I'll feel better if I tease my sister a while." (Mitch Huff)

As a follow up activity, ask students to make up their own quotes for their favorite characters. Post these and allow others to guess the characters. After all students have had an opportunity to play the game, have students identify which quotes they created.

From *The Beverly Cleary Handbook.* © Teacher Ideas Press. (800) 237-6124.

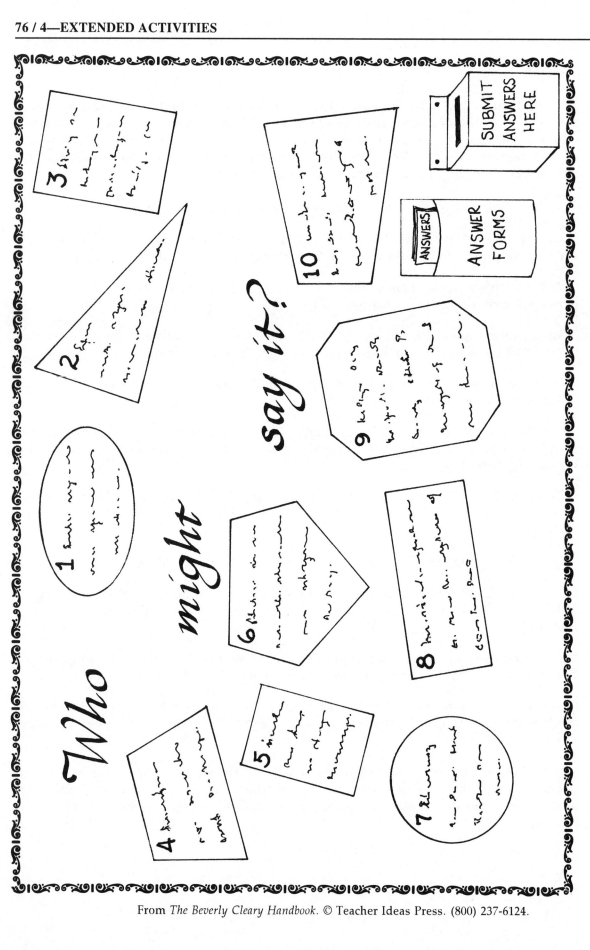

The Battle of Books

The Battle of Books is a game in which teams try to identify titles of books from questions based upon plots, settings, and characters. It can be shaped to fit a cozy little group of friends having fun in the corner of the classroom, or it can involve an entire class, or even several classes at a time. The game can be very simple: two teams of equal numbers of students are alternately asked questions about books. Each team is asked the same number of questions, and points are awarded for correct answers. Audience participation is encouraged and, at the end of the game, the books mentioned should be available for students to read.

A Simplified Version

In the simplest form, no one chooses sides; an imaginary line is drawn, and the class is thus divided into two groups. Details of how the game is played should be determined by the ability of the group, but rules should be kept to a minimum. Questions are asked of one team and then of the other. Sometimes the second team may be given the chance to score if the first team misses. Answers may be given by anyone on the team.

The Traditional Style of Play

In another variation, any group of students may challenge any other group of equal size. Team members do not have to be wonderful readers, just willing. Timekeepers, scorekeepers, and announcers may be selected by the team members or appointed by the teacher. Usually, the teacher acts as the moderator, asking questions and determining the correctness of each answer.

Here are a few simplified rules and guidelines for team play:

1. Each team is asked an equal number of questions. The questions are addressed to the teams alternately, regardless of which team last gave a correct answer. Team one will therefore receive all the odd-numbered questions, and team two all the even-numbered questions.

2. Points are scored by a team that correctly names the book.

3. A team to which a question is addressed has 30 seconds in which to give the answer. If, at the end of 30 seconds, a team is unable to answer a question correctly, the opposing team is allowed the opportunity to give an immediate answer.

Often, when books by a number of different authors are used for questions, bonus points may be awarded if the team can name the author of the book as well as the title.

A Battle Station

If students enjoy this game, set up a Battle Station in the corner of the classroom or library. This station is a box with sets of questions written on 3 by 5 inch index cards. The questions might be arranged in sets: questions on Cleary's picture books in one set, her teenage novels in another, and so on. Small groups of students who have been given permission to spend some free time at the center will enjoy conducting "private" battles. Using scorepads and a timer, if available, might add authenticity to the battles, but these are not necessary for a good time. It might be more fun for students not to keep score or worry about time limits.

A New Approach to the Game

This variation broadens participation, lessens competition, and encourages collaborative learning. The same question is given to all teams at the same time. The teams write down their answers and submit them to the teacher. Any team that answers correctly receives points. Teams should discuss possibilities and come to consensus before submitting an answer. A decision should be made in advance regarding the necessity for correct spelling, but the wording of the answer must follow the title exactly.

An advantage to this approach is that all students on a team cooperate in developing an answer, and there is no room for misinterpretation of a response. It allows for many teams to be involved at the same time; or an entire class can be divided into five or six teams, all playing the same game.

The questions that follow have been arranged into games for the traditional style of play, but they may be used equally well in games based on the newer approach. Many of the following questions were first published in *The Battle of Books* by Joanne Kelly (Teacher Ideas Press, 1990).

Game One

1. Leigh's father has left home, his dog is lost in the mountains, someone is taking all the good things from his lunch box, and his mom still expects him to answer the 20 questions an author has asked him. What book is this?

    ANSWER: *Dear Mr. Henshaw*

2. Keeping his dog out of trouble so he could go salmon fishing with his dad wasn't going to be easy. His dog seemed destined for mischief: he barked at the garbage men and ate Ramona's ice cream cone. What book is this?

    ANSWER: *Henry and Ribsy*

3. First-grader Ramona wants to be spunky and grown up, but she is afraid of the dark in her new bedroom, she upsets the first-grade teacher by crumpling a classmate's artwork, and she embarrasses her big sister. What book is this?

    ANSWER: *Ramona the Brave*

4. A little girl put her doll in a hot oven because she was pretending it was the witch in Hansel and Gretel. She ruined a whole box of apples by taking a single bite out of each one. What book is this?

    ANSWER: *Beezus and Ramona*

5. I am eight years old, take ballet lessons, wear bands on my teeth, and have a secret—I wear woolen underwear. In what book do I appear?

    ANSWER: *Ellen Tebbits*

6. There is a boy who dressed himself all up for trick-or-treating on Halloween. He even put a wolf mask on his dog. He gets more than he planned on when, at one house, a woman who has run out of treats gives him an owl. What book is this?

    ANSWER: *Henry and the Clubhouse*

7. I really see no need to learn that funny way of writing. After all, when I grow up I'll just use a computer to do all the writing I'll ever have to do, and everyone can read that too. In what book do I appear?

    ANSWER: *Muggie Maggie*

8. A boy comes to the aid of his twin sister when the neighborhood bully threatens to eat all the cupcakes she has made for her Girl Scout meetings. What book is this?

    ANSWER: *Mitch and Amy*

9. A mouse runs away from home on his motorcycle because he didn't want to take orders from his uncle. He ended up getting caught by a boy who put him in a cage at a summer camp. What book is this?

    ANSWER: *Runaway Ralph*

10. Ramona is embarrassed when she breaks her hard-boiled egg on her head only to discover she had the wrong egg in her lunch box—and it wasn't hard boiled. What book is this?

    ANSWER: *Ramona Quimby, Age 8*

Game Two

1. A stocking-footed bridesmaid is the heroine of the wedding when she finds a lost wedding ring caught on the heel of the bride's shoe. What book is this?

    ANSWER: *Ramona Forever*

2. The Mountain View Inn has only a few guests, but one changes Ralph's life when he leaves his toy motorcycle parked on a table. Keith had no idea that he'd provided Ralph with an exciting career—miniature motorcyclist! What book is this?

    ANSWER: *The Mouse and the Motorcycle*

3. A boy who likes to cause excitement spit so many spitballs one day that his teacher made him spit spitballs into the trash can for the rest of the day. His mother teaches dancing, and he hates Ellen Tebbits. What book is this?

ANSWER: *Otis Spofford*

4. Mama said that Emily's imagination was always running away with her; something like the way Emily imagined a horse had once run away with Mama. What book is this?

ANSWER: *Emily's Runaway Imagination*

5. A kindergartner hides behind garbage cans because she doesn't want to go to school when there is a substitute teacher. What book is this?

ANSWER: *Ramona the Pest*

6. The day that Henry became a substitute paper boy he met Byron Murphy, the genius who was building a robot, and Henry thought Byron was great. But when the genius takes over the paper route Henry wants, Ramona comes to the rescue. What book is this?

ANSWER: *Henry and the Paper Route*

7. Ralph goes wild over his motorcycle, but his squirmy cousins want too many rides. He runs away to camp, but a boy steals his motorcycle and puts Ralph in a cage! What book is this?

ANSWER: *Runaway Ralph*

8. A boy wraps up a stray dog in paper and string and tries to smuggle him onto a bus. What book is this?

ANSWER: *Henry Huggins*

9. The title of the book is the name of a young tabby cat that has four white paws and lives with Mr. and Mrs. Bricker and their baby, Charles William. What book is this?

ANSWER: *Socks*

10. Ellen is eight years old and she attends Mrs. Spofford's School of Dance. The name of her best friend is Austine Allen, and the name of her worst enemy is Otis Spofford. Ellen's full name is the title of the book. What book is this?

ANSWER: *Ellen Tebbits*

Game Three

1. A boy finds a dog at a drug store; he buys two guppies and ends up with hundreds; his head turns green with paint at Christmas, but his dog turns pink at fair time. What book is this?

ANSWER: *Henry Huggins*

2. Father, who has been the target of his daughter's anti-smoking campaign, puts a sign in her room that reads "A messy room is hazardous to your health." What book is this?

   ANSWER: *Ramona and Her Father*

3. Keith loans a motorcycle to his friend, who uses it to go on wild rides through the corridors of a hotel. When danger threatens his friend, Keith defends him, even though his friend is a mouse. What book is this?

   ANSWER: *The Mouse and the Motorcycle*

4. Leigh has problems! He misses his dad, is angry at the "lunch-box thief," and is sad about being the new kid at school. When he is assigned a letter-writing project, he writes to his favorite author. What book is this?

   ANSWER: *Dear Mr. Henshaw*

5. Who said this?: "I hate Ellen Tebbits. She makes me sick."
   "One day I spit so many spitballs, my teacher made me spit spitballs into the trash basket all day! My mouth got very dry."

   ANSWER: *Otis Spofford*

6. This cat was the center of his household until another pet arrived, but this new creature has a small, wrinkled, furless face and gets lots of attention. The cat is filled with jealousy. This book's title is the cat's name. What book is this?

   ANSWER: *Socks*

7. One of the twins struggles with multiplication tables but loves to read. The other twin has no trouble with math, but struggles to read even "baby books." Though they bicker and tease each other, they help each other overcome problems at home and at school. What book is this?

   ANSWER: *Mitch and Amy*

8. Henry has had his heart set on having a paper route but is sidetracked by four lively kittens, one boy with a robot, and Ramona, the ever present pest of Klickitat Street. What book is this?

   ANSWER: *Henry and the Paper Route*

9. There are three surprises for Beezus and Ramona to deal with: a birth, a death, and a wedding. What book is this?

   ANSWER: *Ramona Forever*

10. Things have gone from bad to worse—Matt has been accused of letting mice run wild at the Mountain View Inn, and all those relatives are greedy for a motorcycle ride! Ralph decides to go to fifth grade with Ryan. What book is this?

    ANSWER: *Ralph S. Mouse*

Game Four

1. When Ralph decides to go to school, Miss Kuchenbacher's fifth-grade class is happy to have him as their guest. They use him to launch a study of rodents, but a newspaper reports a mouse plague at the school! What book is this?

    ANSWER: *Ralph S. Mouse*

2. Henry removes this dog's collar and tags so that the dog can scratch a flea. Now, with an accidental tap of the paw on the button that controls the car window, this city dog is free! This dog becomes lost on an adventure. What book is this?

    ANSWER: *Ribsy*

3. Ramona knows that she has the answer to the family financial crisis: She'll pretend that she has fluffy blond hair and is cute and lovable. Then she'll make a million dollars. What book is this?

    ANSWER: *Ramona and Her Father*

4. A girl washes a horse with Clorox to turn it into a snow-white steed. She also helps her mother start the first library in the town of Pitchfork. What book is this?

    ANSWER: *Emily's Runaway Imagination*

5. At last Henry has his very own bike! Beezus had bid on it at the bike auction and it took all of Henry's $4.04 savings to buy it. He thinks it is worth every penny until he sees that Beezus bought a girl's bike for him. What book is this?

    ANSWER: *Henry and Beezus*

6. Ramona has had it! She has decided to run away! Nobody likes her at home, and now Mrs. Rudge has told Mother about the pajamas at school. Now Mother is so eager to get rid of her that she offers to help Ramona pack her suitcase. What book is this?

    ANSWER: *Ramona and Her Mother*

7. A boy asks a girl for a date—to go with him to the annual volunteer Lover's Point Weed Pull. Some people might think that this is a strange sort of a date, but he doesn't, and neither does she. What book is this?

    ANSWER: *Strider*

8. A boy being silly, holding a dark lock of hair under his nose like a mustache. But no one is laughing. Everyone is horrified because, just moments ago, the hair under his nose had been Ellen Tebbits's pigtail! What book is this?

    ANSWER: *Otis Spofford*

9. "Sit here for the present Ramona," said Miss Binney. "A present!" thought Ramona. Nobody had told her that she would be getting a present the first day of kindergarten! What book is this?

ANSWER: *Ramona the Pest*

10. "Ramona Quimby, stop pestering Henry Huggins on his paper route!" Sheriff Bud said. Ramona stared at the television set in wonder. Henry must be a friend of her favorite television star! What book is this?

ANSWER: *Henry and the Clubhouse*

Game Five

1. Henry takes a ride in a bathtub and pretends that he is the President of the United States on the way to the White House. His fun stops when he remembers that he has newspapers to deliver. What book is this?

ANSWER: *Henry and the Clubhouse*

2. Whose dog is that running out on the football field? Look! He tripped up the runner before he made that winning touchdown! Taylor High School wins the game, all because of a dog. Who is the dog and what book is this?

ANSWER: *Ribsy*

3. It was a quiet Saturday morning when a knock came at the front door, and in trooped the entire nursery school, ready for a party. The party refreshments are apple sauce and worm sandwiches. What book is this?

ANSWER: *Beezus and Ramona*

4. Ramona shocks her family when she announces that she is so mad, she's going to say a bad word. "Guts!" she hollers, "Guts! Guts! Guts!" But her family isn't at all upset—in fact, they all laugh. What book is this?

ANSWER: *Ramona the Brave*

5. Ralph, a mouse, is in trouble at his home in the Mountain View Inn. He decides to find a new home at the school that Ryan, the housekeeper's son, attends. What book is this?

ANSWER: *Ralph S. Mouse*

6. They worked out a joint-custody arrangement for the dog they found at the beach, but after a while it didn't work very well. The dog knew which one of the boys he really wanted to be with all of the time. What book is this?

ANSWER: *Strider*

7. Henry thinks that he is rich because he's found 49 boxes of bubble gum, and each box has 300 bubble gum balls in it. When the kids at school won't buy it all, Henry has to turn to Beezus for help. What book is this?

ANSWER: *Henry and Beezus*

8. A stubborn third-grader has to learn to read cursive writing because she wants to be able to read the notes the teacher sends to the principal and other teachers. She suspects that the notes are about her. What book is this?

    ANSWER: *Muggie Maggie*

9. This week, hard-boiled eggs are the fad in the third grade. The best way of cracking the egg is to whack it against your head. When Ramona whacks, something slimy runs down her face. Her egg is raw! What book is this?

    ANSWER: *Ramona Quimby, Age 8*

10. He kept his dog out of trouble for one month so that he could go salmon fishing with his father. But when they finally go after the Big Chinook, the dog causes more mischief than ever. What book is this?

    ANSWER: *Henry and Ribsy*

Battles Designed with Thinking Skills in Mind

Traditionally, the answers to Battle questions have been titles of books, and students are required to recall facts about characters, plots, and settings. There is, however, another level of questioning that may be employed in situations where there is interest in developing critical thinking skills. The newer, collaborative form of this game lends itself especially well to this form of question. Here are some examples:

1a. What do the following towns have in common?
    Portland, Oregon
    Pacific Grove, California
    Pitchfork, Oregon

    ANSWER: All three are settings for books by Beverly Cleary.
    Portland—The Henry and Ramona books (and others)
    Pacific Grove—*Dear Mr. Henshaw, Strider*
    Pitchfork—*Emily's Runaway Imagination*

1b. One of these three towns is quite different than the other two. Which one is it, and why is it different?

    ANSWER: Pitchfork is a fictional town, the other two are real places. (Credit might also be given for noticing that Pacific Grove is in California, while the other two are in Oregon.)

2a. What do the following characters have in common?
    Ramona Quimby
    Leigh Botts
    Otis Spofford

    ANSWER: Their mothers all work outside the home.

2b. One of these characters has a different situation at home. Who is it and what is the difference?

ANSWER: Ramona is the only one with a sibling, and the only one who lives with both her parents.

3. Here are four characters from Cleary books: Picky-picky, Ribsy, Strider, and Socks. In which of the following shows would all of them be likely to perform?
   horse show
   dog show
   puppet show
   pet show
   quiz show

ANSWER: A pet show.

4. Which book does not belong and why?
   Ramona Forever
   Mitch and Amy
   Muggie Maggie
   Runaway Ralph
   Ribsy
   Socks

ANSWER: *Runaway Ralph* is the only book in which animals talk. It is the only fantasy.

5. How many similarities can you find between Beverly Cleary and Ramona Quimby?

ANSWERS (there are several other points that could be made):
   They are both female.
   They both lived in the same neighborhood in Portland, Oregon.
   They both had trouble adjusting to first grade.
   Both their fathers were out of work for quite a long time.

Bookmarks and Buttons

The bookmarks and buttons that are included here may be reproduced freely. Use them just as they are, adapt them to fit program needs, or use them as inspiration for creating original artwork. Personalize the bookmarks and buttons by inserting student and school names. They might even be enlarged and used as bulletin board material.

Bookmark and Button References

Page 87
1. Any of the Henry or Ramona books.
2. *A Girl from Yamhill* or biographical information given here.
3. Various titles.
4. *Beezus and Ramona.*
5. Ribsy.

Page 88
1. Beverly Cleary.
2. Beverly Cleary.
3. Leigh Botts.
4. Ramona Quimby.
5. *Ralph S. Mouse.*

Page 89
1. Books by Cleary are great!
2. *Strider.*
3. *Socks.*
4. *Mouse and the Motorcycle, Runaway Ralph, Ralph S. Mouse.*
5. *Dear Mr. Henshaw.*

Page 90
1. Ramona.
2. *Henry and Ribsy.*
3. by Cleary.
4. *Henry and the Clubhouse.*
5. I love stories of Klickitat Street by Beverly Cleary.

(Text continues on page 91.)

WHO AM I?

I gathered up papers and brought them all home. I ate a big hunk of a girl's ice cream cone. I defended our garbage so men couldn't take it. And I rained a touchdown before he could make it.

Does the first bite of an apple always taste the best? Read Beezus and Ramona by Beverly Cleary to find out what Ramona thinks.

HENRY HUGGINS ■ RAMONA THE PEST ■ ELLEN TEBBITS ■ MITCH AND AMY ■ HENRY AND THE CLUBHOUSE ■ BEEZUS AND RAMONA ■ SOCKS ■ all written by Beverly Cleary! RUNAWAY RALPH ■ OTIS SPOFFORD ■ RIBSY ■ THE MOUSE AND THE MOTORCYCLE ■ STRIDER ■ DEAR MR. HENSHAW

In what Oregon town did the author of Ramona the Pest grow up?
ANSWER: (use a mirror) PORTLAND

KLICKITAT
On Klickitat Street A bunch of friends meet, Where Henry's at home— And Ribsy can roam.
CAN YOU NAME ONE OF THE BOOKS ABOUT KLICKITAT STREET?

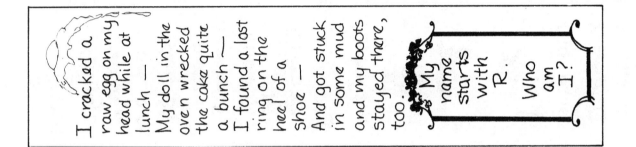

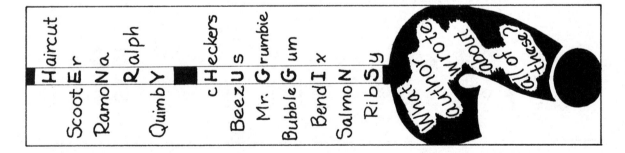

From *The Beverly Cleary Handbook.* © Teacher Ideas Press. (800) 237-6124.

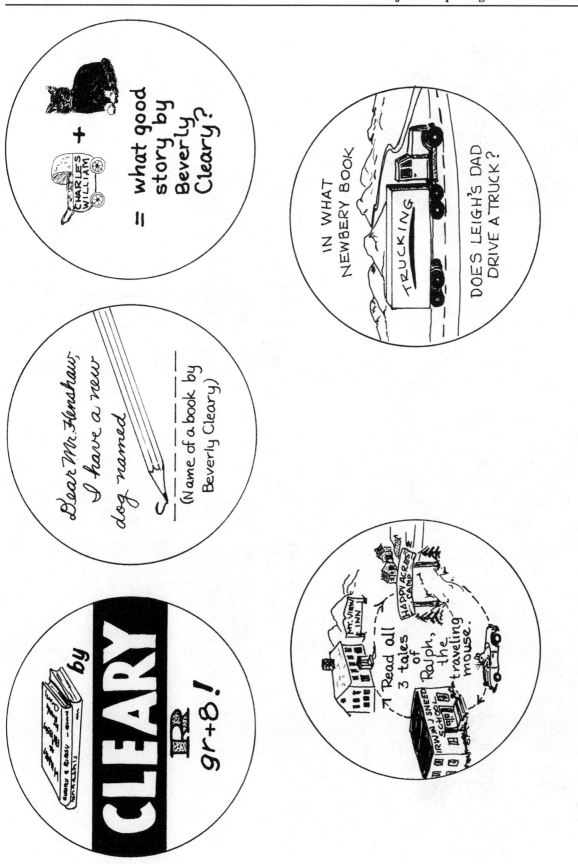

INDEPENDENT ACTIVITIES

Map Activities

The map on the following page represents Portland, Oregon and the northeast Portland neighborhood where Beverly Cleary lived for much of her childhood. The actual streets and places shown here were used by Cleary in creating the settings for many of her fiction books. Both the real names and their fictional counterparts are given in the map key. Use this map to complete the activities that follow.

KEY
(NAMES USED IN BOOKS ARE GIVEN IN PARENTHESES)

1. LAURELHURST PARK
2. LAURELHURST SCHOOL (CEDARHURST ELEMENTARY SCHOOL)
3. LLOYD CENTER SHOPPING MALL
4. HOLLYWOOD THEATER (LAURELWOOD THEATER)
5. KIENOWS SUPERMARKET (A NEW SUPERMARKET)
6. GAS STATION AT 33RD AND BROADWAY (AL'S THRIFTY SERVICE STATION)
7. FERNWOOD SCHOOL (GLENWOOD SCHOOL)
8. HOLLYWOOD BRANCH OF MULTNOMAH COUNTY LIBRARY (GLENWOOD OR ROSE CITY LIBRARY)
9. HOLLYWOOD YMCA
10. WESTMINSTER PRESBYTERIAN CHURCH
11. TILLAMOOK STREET
12. GRANT PARK, HOME OF THE BEVERLY CLEARY SCULPTURE GARDEN FOR CHILDREN
13. KNOTT STREET
14. KLICKITAT STREET
15. BEAUMONT MIDDLE SCHOOL (ROSEMONT SCHOOL)
16. LOMBARD STREET
17. THE COLUMBIA RIVER
18. THE INTERSTATE BRIDGE

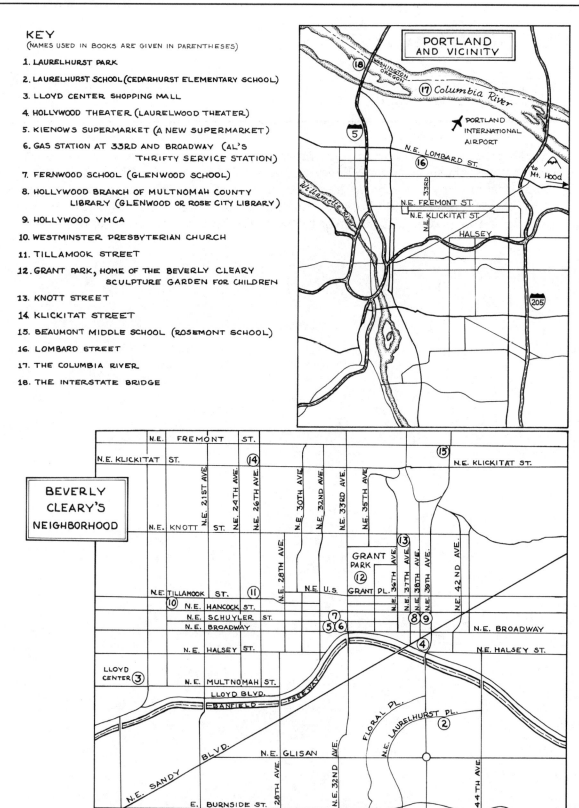

From *The Beverly Cleary Handbook*. © Teacher Ideas Press. (800) 237-6124.

Find These Story Places

On this map of northeast Portland, find the following places. Write the number for the correct place in the space in front of each question. You may want to refer to figures 3.1–3.15 (pages 50–60) for more help.

1. _____ Beezus and Henry went to elementary school here, and Ramona attended kindergarten and the first and second grades.

2. _____ While Henry was stuck in a car on top of the grease rack here, Ribsy stole a policeman's lunch.

3. _____ Ellen and Austine took Otis's shoes and boots while he was ice-skating on this lake.

4. _____ Ramona was in Mrs. Whaley's third grade here.

5. _____ Henry goes swimming here every week, and he found Ribsy at the drugstore on the corner near here.

6. _____ Ramona and her family go to church here, and Ramona and her friends were in a Christmas program here.

7. _____ Ellen and Otis go to school here.

8. _____ This is the place where Beezus and Ramona return *Big Steve*, Ramona's favorite book.

9. _____ Henry, his friends, and his family go to the movies here.

10. _____ This is the spot where Uncle Hobart took Ramona, Beezus, Willa Jean, and Howie to pick out clothes for his wedding to Aunt Bea.

11. _____ Ramona got stuck in the mud in the construction site of this store across from her school.

12. _____ This is the place where statues of Henry, Ribsy, and Ramona can be found.

Find the Street

1. Draw a green line on the street where Henry, Beezus, and Ramona live.

2. Draw a red line on the street where Mr. Capper, the man who hires paperboys, lives.

3. Draw a blue line on the street where Ellen Tebbits lives.

4. Draw a purple line on the street where Henry rode in a bathtub.

5. Draw a circle around two places Ramona and her father drew on "The Longest Picture in the World."

Hidden Names

Hidden in the following sentences are the names of these characters from books by Beverly Cleary:

Beatrice	Emily	Leigh	Otis	Ramona
Ellen	Henry	Maggie	Ralph	Socks

Underline the names as you find them in the sentences below, then write the name in the spaces after each sentence. The first puzzle has been solved for you.

1. Weight lifting can <u>be a trice</u>ps builder.   <u>B E A T R I C E</u>

2. Most people think this book has a swell ending.   _____

3. She preferred handkerchiefs to tissues.   _____

4. How many kids can cram on a bus?   _____

5. I like my ham sandwiches best when rye bread is used along with Swiss cheese.

   _____

6. In the new shopping mall, eighty stores proudly opened their doors.

   _____

7. When the girls waded in the creek, they took off their shoes and socks.

   _____

8. Texas A & M college students call players on their football team "Aggies."

   _____

9. He spent an hour alphabetizing animals.   _____

10. I told them! I, lying here on this bed, have the chicken pox!   _____

Scrambled Titles

How many of the mixed-up words below can you unscramble to make titles of Beverly Cleary books? The first one has been done for you.

1. Leysi'm Wyranua Notigaminia <u>EMILY'S RUNAWAY IMAGINATION</u>

2. Skocs _____

3. Sirby _____

4. Ryhen Gunighs _____

5. Tosi Dorfpofs _____

6. Nomara Bimquy, Gae 8 _____ , _____

7. Manaro het Raveb _____

8. Yrneh adn Sybir _____

9. Het Somue dan eth Rocmetcoly _____

10. Nelle Betsbit _____

Writing Activities

Now You're the Author

Complete one or more of the following activities:

1. Imagine that Leigh Botts had just enrolled at Fernwood School and was assigned to the same classroom as Henry and Beezus. Describe how you think they would behave in this situation. Do you believe that they would be friends? How would they get to know one another? Do you think there would be any problems? For example, would Ribsy and Strider be friendly, or would they have a fight? Leigh doesn't have a bike or a father at home. Would that make a difference? Use your imagination and write one or more paragraphs to tell what you think would happen.

2. Mitch and Amy Huff have moved into Otis and Ellen's neighborhood. Amy is taking lessons at the Spofford School of Dance, and Mitch has been assigned to Otis and Ellen's class. Will Mitch and Otis like each other? Will Austine and Ellen try to be friends with Amy? Do you think there might be any trouble? Write at least one paragraph telling what you think might happen.

3. The Bricker family, including Charles William and Socks, have taken a vacation in the California mountains. They have decided to stay at a quaint old hotel named The Mountain View Inn. As they cross the lobby, Mrs. Bricker, holding Socks, tells Mr. Bricker, who is carrying Charles William, that she must be seeing things. She thought she saw a mouse driving a motorcycle hide behind the television set. Write one paragraph or more telling what happens next.

4. Choose four characters from Beverly Cleary's books. Predict what each of them will be doing 10 years after their stories end. Write at least one paragraph of prediction for each of the four characters.

    Here is an example:

    Maggie Schultz (of *Muggie Maggie*) is now 18 years old. She has just graduated from high school, where she was an outstanding student with the highest grades in her class. She was editor of the high school newspaper and a star on the track team, where she was known for her endurance and speed. In her spare time she earns money by doing expert calligraphy (fancy writing) for wedding invitations. Her teachers attribute her success to her active curiosity and stubborn determination. Maggie says that she wants to study journalism in college because she likes to find out what's happening, and because she enjoys writing.

5. Write a description of a Cleary character but don't give his or her name. Describe the character's appearance, feelings, ideas, and things he or she did. What do other characters think of him or her? Post your description where your classmates can read it, and see if they can correctly identify the character.

Here is an example:

This boy enjoys building things and fixing things. He is a little chunky because he really likes to eat. He doesn't like to dress up in good clothes. He is a no-nonsense boy who never exaggerates, doesn't talk unless he has something important to say, and he doesn't have much of a sense of humor or imagination. Luckily he has a good friend with plenty of both. He is bothered by his pesty little sister, and he admires his rich uncle. He once built a two-wheeler bike out of a tricycle. Who is he?

(ANSWER: Howie Kemp)

6. Write a newspaper account of some event in a book by Beverly Cleary. Use this plan:

Write a headline that will make people want to read your article.

Paragraph 1—Tell the specific facts—Who, What, Where, and When.

Paragraph 2—Add important details.

Paragraph 3—Add other details that are interesting but not as important.

Here is an example:

Boy Catches Huge Fish with Bare Hands

History was made near the mouth of the Umptucca River Saturday when Henry Huggins, a 10-year-old boy from Portland, pulled a 29 pound Chinook salmon from a stream close to the Umptucca. Huggins had no fishing tackle with him when he encountered the fish, so he simply caught it and dragged it out of the water with his bare hands.

"My dog, Ribsy, helped me find the Chinook," said Huggins. "He barked to let me know it was there. I just kept pushing the fish into shallower and shallower water until he couldn't get away from me. Then I managed to get a hand into his gills, but he was flopping around so much I couldn't pull him out. Then a man came along and hit him hard with a piece of wood, and I picked him up."

That gentleman confirmed that Huggins had waded into the stream and caught the fish by himself. It was weighed at *Mike's Place*, a nearby boathouse. Huggins related that although he had started the day fishing from a rental boat with his father and a neighbor, a disturbance involving his dog had forced him to leave the boat. "I found the fish as Ribsy and I were exploring the shoreline and watching the fishermen," Huggins related to this reporter as his father took a photo of the proud boy.

7. Beverly Cleary has written books that have settings in almost every place she has lived, from her very youngest years in Yamhill, Oregon (*Emily's Runaway Imagination*), to a town near her present home of Carmel, California (*Dear Mr. Henshaw* and *Strider*). She frequently sets the action of her story in real places within these cities and uses real facts about these places as part of her stories, as she did with the Butterfly Trees in *Dear Mr. Henshaw*. Think of a park, a shopping mall, a school, or some other place you know well. Use it as a setting for a short story, or write a paragraph of factual information about the place.

Now You Can Be a Poet

Do one or more of these projects:

1. Write a limerick about an event or a character in one of the Cleary books. A limerick is a silly verse made up of five lines. The first, second, and fifth lines rhyme, and the third and fourth lines rhyme.

   Here is an example:

   > There was a small mouse from an inn,
   > Who gave rides to a dozen small kin;
   > He said, "They're a load!
   > I'm off down the road
   > With my cycle, my freedom I'll win."

2. Make up a cinquain. A cinquain is a five-line poem; all five lines are about one topic. The form is like this:

   Line 1—Two words or two syllables that tell the topic.
   Line 2—Four syllables that describe the topic.
   Line 3—Six syllables that describe some action.
   Line 4—Eight syllables that indicate some feeling.
   Line 5—Two syllables that are a synonym for the topic.

   Here is an example:

   > Ribsy
   > Middle-sized dog
   > Chasing after Henry
   > Loves to eat and run and play ball
   > Loyal

3. Write a character poem following this pattern:

   Line 1—Name of character.
   Line 2—Three words that describe the character.
   Line 3—A relative or friend of the character.
   Line 4—"Who likes . . ." (something or someone the character likes).
   Line 5—"Who wants . . ." (something the character wants).
   Line 6—"Who really . . ."
   Line 7—"Resident of . . ."
   Line 8—Words that describe the character.

Here is an example:

Otis Spofford
Clever mischief maker
Son of Valerie Spofford
Who likes to stir up excitement
Who wants Mutt the rat
Who really didn't mean to cut Ellen's hair
Resident of Portland
Rambunctious boy.

4. Construct a haiku, a type of three-line Japanese poem that is usually about something in nature.

Line 1—five syllables.
Line 2—seven syllables.
Line 3—five syllables.

Here is an example:

Strider the lost dog
Alone and hungry and scared
Waiting on the beach

5. Try an acrostic. Write the name of a character, a setting, or a title from one of the Cleary books, but write it vertically, and fill in each line with words and phrases that begin with the first letter of the line and describe the subject in some way.

Here is an example that is both a title and two characters:

Made his own skateboard
Is really a good kid
Teases his sister
Confronts Alan, the bully
Hates reading "baby books"

A set of twins
Never refuse to help each other
Determined to be independent

Always loves to read
Multiplication is hard for her
Young cellist

Turning Fact into Fiction

Authors often use things that have happened to them or to people they have known as the basis for stories they create many years later. In *The Girl from Yamhill*, the book that Beverly Cleary wrote about her childhood, she tells of many happenings in her past that are very much like episodes in books she has written. In the first column below are some notes from her autobiography. The page numbers at the end of each segment refer to pages in *The Girl from Yamhill*. In the next column is a listing of chapters in her fiction books that match those incidents. Match the notes in the first column to the title/chapter headings in the second column. An example is given below.

Episodes in *The Girl from Yamhill*

1. Having been told that the earth was round, she set out to walk around it starting in the barnyard of the Yamhill farm, over the fences and across the fields, intending to end up just where she began. (pp. 30–31) (This is from Cleary's real-life story.)

The Facts

2. When they lived in Yamhill, her mother told her that there was a pot of gold at the end of the rainbow, so the next time a rainbow appeared, she took off in search of gold. (p. 32)

3. As a little girl on the Yamhill family farm, she sat under the apple tree taking one bite from a fallen apple, throwing the rest away, then biting into another because she thought the first bite from an apple tastes best. (pp. 23–44)

4. Her father lost his job and was out of work for a long time. The family had little extra money, so they had to watch every penny they spent. (pp. 173–75+)

5. A favorite Portland game was "Brick Factory," where the children pounded old bricks into dust. (p. 71)

6. A boy in her class named Ralph once stirred up some excitement by eating garlic and making the whole classroom smell terrible. (p. 122)

Episodes in Fiction Books

1. *Beezus and Ramona*, chapter 4 (In this chapter, Beezus is afraid that Ramona has set out to try to walk around the world because she just learned that the world is round.)

The Fiction

CAUTION: There are too many books listed in this column. Some have no match!

_____ *Ramona the Brave*, chapter 3

_____ *Ramona and Her Father*, chapter 1

_____ *Otis Spofford*, chapter 2

_____ *Ramona the Brave*, chapter 5

_____ *Beezus and Ramona*, chapter 4

_____ *Beezus and Ramona*, chapter 2

More Facts

1. Every morning first grade began with a mysterious song about the "dawnzer lee light." (p. 76)

2. With her friends on Halsey Street in Portland, she made tin-can stilts out of two-pound coffee cans. They clanked around the block yelling "Pie-face" at other children. (p. 71)

3. A first-grade classmate who lived in her neighborhood made fun of her for naming her doll after a tractor. (p. 80)

4. In an unhappy incident, her third-grade teacher called her a "nuisance." (p. 100)

5. No matter how she argued, her mother made her wear woolen under-wear to school. (p. 116)

6. She bragged to classmates that she had ridden lots of horses. She really had only ridden on a farm horse behind her father and on a rented pony at the beach. (pp. 127, 140)

7. She fell in love with a boy named Johnny and chased him around the school. (p. 95)

More Fiction

_____ *Ramona Quimby, Age 8*, chapter 3

_____ *Ellen Tebbits*, chapter 4

_____ *Ramona the Pest*, chapter 2

_____ *Ramona and Her Father*, chapter 5

_____ *Henry and Ribsy*, chapter 2

_____ *Ramona the Pest*, chapter 3

_____ *Ellen Tebbits*, chapter 1

_____ *Ramona and Her Mother*, chapter 5

_____ *Ramona the Pest*, chapter 8

Something to Think About

Beverly Cleary has said that when she was a child she was very much like Ellen Tebbits. Given the evidence from the comparison charts, do you agree? If not, what character is more like Cleary as a child?

Now You *Try It*

THE FACTS

In the space below, write about something that happened to you. *List* the following information:

1. What was the single most important thing that happened in the incident?
2. Who was involved?
3. Where did it happen?
4. When did it happen? Include the time of day and the season of the year.

Try to remember as much as you can about how you felt at the time. Were you happy, embarrassed, confused, surprised, or sad? How did other people who were involved in the incident act? Could you tell how they felt? Tell something of the sights, sounds, and smells you recall. Be sure to tell what happened at the beginning, the middle, and the end, and include time-order words such as "First," "Then," "Next," and "Last."

THE FICTION

Now take the facts you have written above and turn them into a story. You may want to change the characters in some way: make them younger or older or turn them from boys to girls (or the other way around). You might want to change the time of year or the place where the action happens. It's all up to you!

Activities for Individual Titles

Muggie Maggie

What's Wrong Here?

In each sentence below are one or two words that are incorrect. Underline the incorrect word. Rewrite the paragraph correctly on the lines below.

Muggie Maggie is about a girl who is in the fourth grade. She doesn't want to learn to write in printing. Her teacher, Mrs. Leeper, sent her to the school office to talk to the cook. Maggie was made library monitor. She carried books to other teachers. She couldn't read the books until she learned to read printing. She practiced at home and soon was able to read and write printing, and she could read the books, too. When she read a book written by the principal, she found that it was about her!

Rewrite Maggie's story the way it really happened:

_____

_____

_____

_____

_____

_____

_____

_____

_____

_____

_____

Beezus and Ramona

The TOP TEN Best and Worst Things About Being an Older Sister

Beezus is the oldest of the Quimby girls. Sometimes she likes that, but often she doesn't like having a little sister at all. Pretend that you are Beezus when you make the lists below.

Make a list of the five best things about being the oldest Quimby daughter. Number them in order: 1 (best) to 5 (worst)

_____

_____

_____

_____

_____

_____

Now make a list of the five worst things about being the oldest daughter. Number them in order: 1 (worst worst) to 5 (least worst).

_____

_____

_____

_____

_____

_____

Socks

Mega-Movies, the famous Hollywood film company, is going to make a movie of the book *Socks*. It will be a full-length animated cartoon, but will follow the plot of the book very closely. Mrs. Cleary will oversee the production of the film.

The producers have planned a large and expensive advertising campaign to announce the opening of the film so that it will entice large audiences of young movie-goers. You have been hired to write an advertisement that will tell people about the film, and your job isn't easy. You must make the film sound so exciting that no one will want to miss it, but you have a very small space for your advertisement: it must be 20 words (or less).

Write your 20-word advertisement for the movie *Socks* in the space below:

_____

_____

_____

_____

_____

_____

_____

In the space below, set your ad into a picture or design that will attract the attention of newspaper readers:

Ribsy

Henry did many things to try to bring Ribsy back home. Ribsy did many things to try to get back home. Some things were successful and helped to bring Ribsy home, and some things didn't help at all. Listed below are a number of actions taken by Henry and a number taken by Ribsy. For each of them, put an X in the column for "Worked" if you think the action helped bring him home, or in the "Useless" column if you think it didn't help. Be sure you carefully consider all the things that happened as a result of the action.

ACTION   WORKED   USELESS

1. Ribsy jumped out of the Dingley's car and ran away, still smelling like violets.

2. Henry placed an advertisement in the paper for a lost dog.

3. Ribsy followed a mailman onto a bus.

4. Ribsy chased a squirrel around a classroom.

5. Ribsy played in a high school football game.

6. Henry telephoned Joe Saylor.

7. Ribsy ran away from Joe, looking for Henry.

8. Ribsy taught Larry how to play ball.

9. Henry and his family drove around looking for Ribsy.

10. Ribsy barked and barked when he was caught on the fire escape.

Henry and the Club House

As a result of Henry's successful career as a paper boy, the *Journal* has made him carrier of the month and will run a feature article about him in the Sunday paper. They will have testimonials from his customers and interview Henry, too. To be prepared for the interview, the editor has asked Henry to prepare a list of the things he likes best about being a paper boy and the things he likes the least. Pretend you are Henry, and fill out the charts below.

The Best Things About Being a Paper Boy

_____

_____

_____

_____

_____

The Worst Things About Being a Paper Boy

_____

_____

_____

_____

_____

Put a check mark beside your favorite item on the "best" list and a check next to your least favorite on the "worst" list. In the spaces below, explain your choices.

Henry's "Best of the Best"_____

_____

Henry's "Worst of the Worst"_____

_____

Runaway Ralph—
A Mouse on His Own

In this book, Ralph yearns to be independent, to be free to make decisions for himself. Sometimes he was able to accomplish that goal. There were other times when events led to trouble, and he needed a little help from others. Below is a list of those characters in the book that might have helped Ralph when he was in a tight spot.

Hint #1: Not all of them were helpful in this book, although they may have been in other stories about Ralph.

Hint #2: Some of them didn't intend to help him at all!

Uncle Lester	Matt	Sam	gopher	Chum
Catso	Garf	Aunt Jill	Lana	Karen

Here are some of the problems Ralph encountered in the book. After each one, write the name of the character that helped him solve the problem. If you decide that Ralph helped himself through a particular crisis, write his name in that space.

1. Ralph can't get his motorcycle down the front steps of the Inn._____

2. Ralph is chased by Sam, who tries to keep him out of Happy Acres Camp._____

3. Catso uses Ralph to teach the kittens how to terrorize a mouse._____

4. Ralph was lonely in his cage and wanted someone to talk with._____

5. Ralph was locked in a cage and had to escape._____

6. Garf has the motorcycle, and Ralph wants it back._____

7. Ralph can't drag Karen's watch to her sleeping bag._____

8. Ralph must return to the Mountain View Inn before winter comes._____

Dear Mr. Henshaw

Mr. Henshaw sends Leigh a postcard with a picture of snowy mountain lakes on it, and he gives Leigh some advice about keeping a diary. That same day, Leigh received a postcard from his dad telling him he would phone him soon. That postcard had a picture of some grain elevators.

Here is a sample postcard. Write a message to Leigh and tell him a little about yourself. Next, give him a bit of advice about how you think he might deal with one of his problems. Don't forget to address the postcard with his name, city, and state. Can you find the ZIP code for his hometown in an almanac or ZIP code directory?

Here is the picture side of your postcard to Leigh. Draw a picture of something important or beautiful in your hometown.

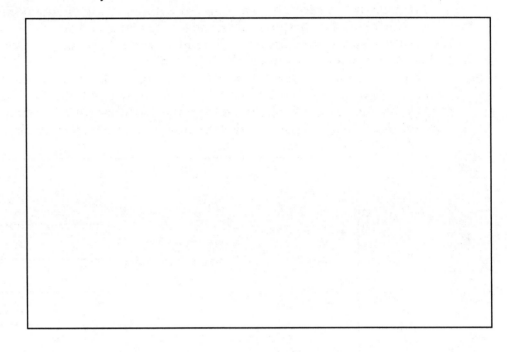

Ralph S. Mouse

Miss Kuckenbacker was the kind of teacher that could turn almost anything into a class project, and she loved to find learning experiences for her students. Now she has suggested that students should think over their recent experiences in Room 5 and record their feelings about them in some way. Pretend that you are a member of Miss Kuckenbacker 's class and complete her assignment.

Here is a list of important events that have occurred in Room 5 since Ralph arrived:

_____ 1. Ralph runs the maze in an unusual way.

_____ 2. The *Cucaracha Voice* prints an untrue story.

_____ 3. The class writes letters to the editor.

_____ 4. The superintendent conducts an investigation.

_____ 5. The newspaper prints an apology.

_____ 6. Other (You may think of something else to write in here.)

Put an X in the space in front of the event that you think was the most important or the funniest. Now design a bumper sticker to illustrate how you feel about that event.

Here is an example:

> # LOVE A MOUSE

Design your bumper sticker in this space:

Ramona and Her Mother

In this story, Ramona and Beezus each have many problems about which they are uneasy. Complete a list for each girl. A few examples have been given for each.

Ramona's Problems

1. Beezus is Mother's girl and I'm not.

2. Willa Jean is like I was at her age.

_____

_____

_____

_____

_____

Beezus's Problems

1. I want to get my haircut in a beauty shop.

2. Daddy doesn't like his job.

_____

_____

_____

_____

_____

Write any problems the girls share below:

_____

_____

_____

_____

_____

_____

_____

_____

Draw a star in front of every problem that was solved by the end of the book.

Rebuses

A rebus is a puzzle that combines pictures with letter sounds to form words or phrases. The five rebuses that follow are all based on Beverly Cleary and her books. Give them a try.

The following rebuses were first published in *Rebuses for Readers* by Pat Martin, Joanne Kelly, and Kay V. Grabow (Teacher Ideas Press, 1992).

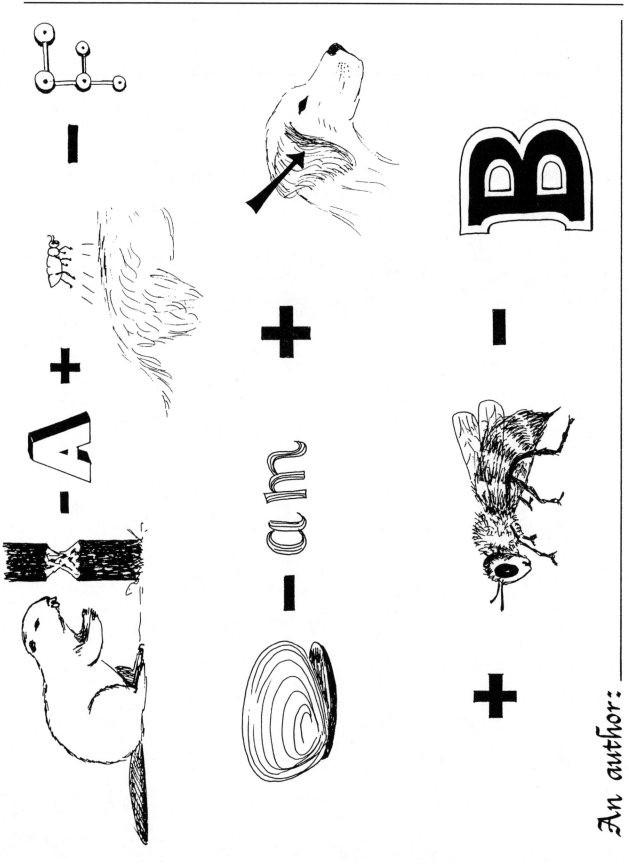

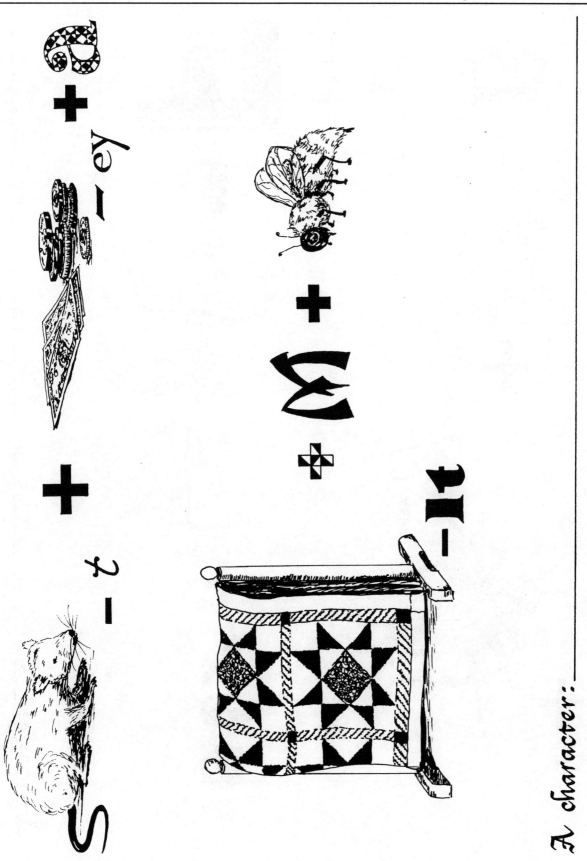

A character: _____

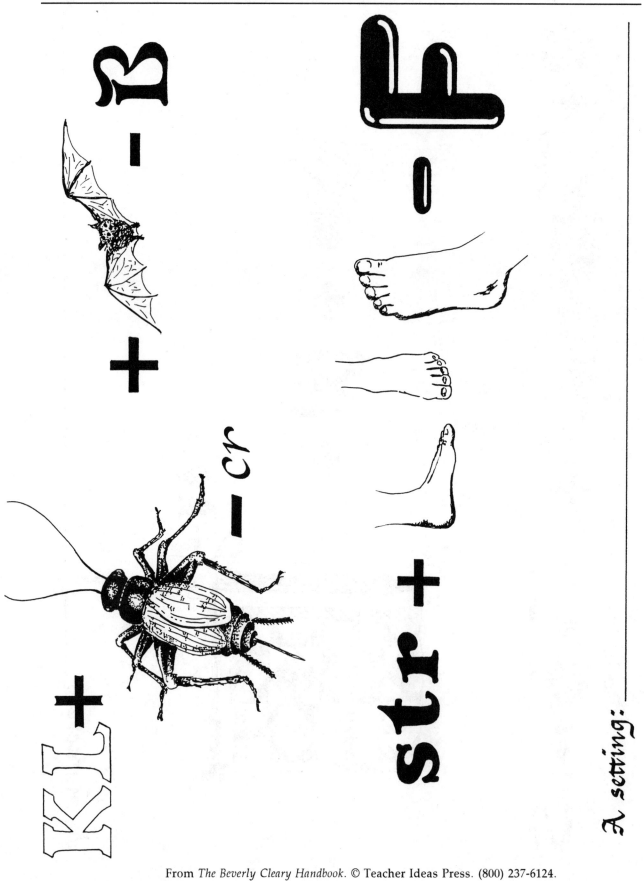

A setting: _____

A title: _____

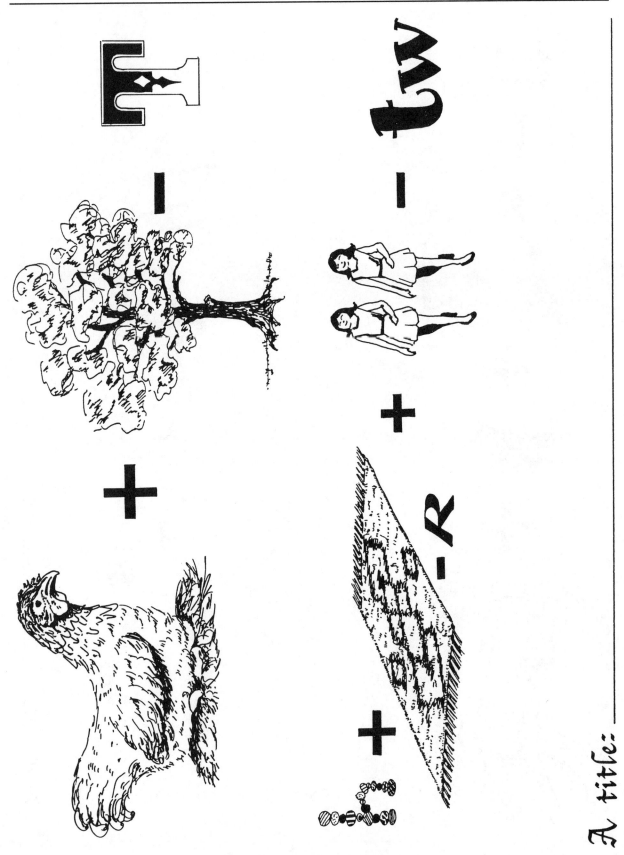

Crossword #1: Ribsy

```
  ┌───┬───┬───┬───┬───┬───┬───┐
  │   │   │ 1 │   │ R │   │   │
  ├───┼───┼───┼───┼───┼───┼───┤
  │   │   │ 2 │   │ I │   │ + │
  ├───┼───┼───┼───┼───┼───┼───┤
  │ 3 │   │   │   │ B │   │   │
  ├───┼───┼───┼───┼───┼───┼───┤
  │   │ 4 │   │   │ S │   │   │
  ├───┼───┼───┼───┼───┼───┼───┤
  │ 5 │   │   │   │ Y │   │   │
  └───┴───┴───┴───┴───┴───┴───┘
```

ACROSS CLUES

1. Ribsy wouldn't allow the trash collectors to take this from the Huggin's house.
2. When Ribsy was lost, Henry found him stuck on a _____ + _____ .
3. Ribsy got his picture on the front page of the Journal when he played in a _____ game.
4. Ribsy made Henry mad because he brought home all of these that Henry had just delivered.
5. Ribsy's "boy."

Crossword #2: Henry

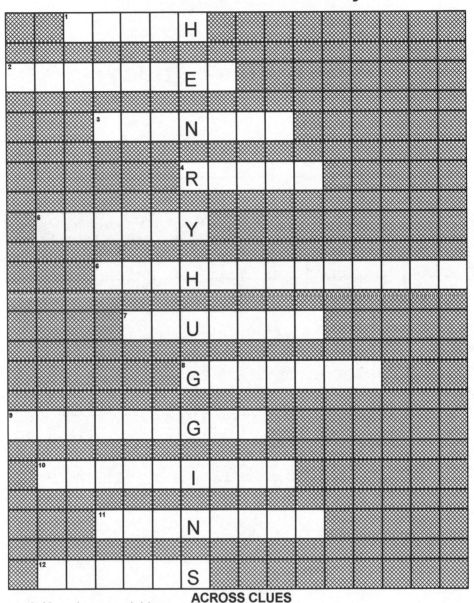

ACROSS CLUES

1. Henry's new neighbor.
2. The man in charge of neighborhood paper routes.
3. The kind of salmon Henry caught.
4. The name of Henry's dog.
5. The author of Henry Huggins.
6. Henry collects 1,331 of these in one evening in Grant Park.
7. The newspaper Henry delivers.
8. Henry started out with a pair of these but soon had hundreds in jars.
9. When Henry finds 49 boxes of this, he thinks he is rich.
10. The street where Henry lives.
11. Henry's school.
12. Henry's good and sensible friend.

Crossword #3: The Author

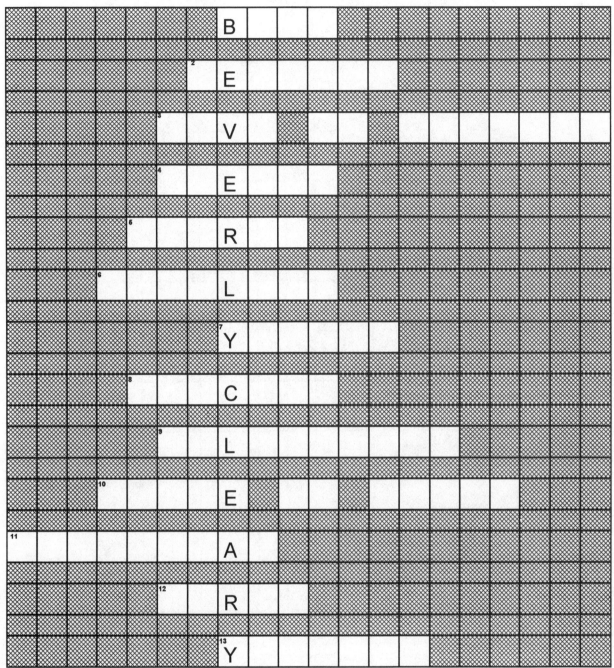

ACROSS CLUES

1. Beverly Cleary's maiden (before she was married) name.
2. An award she won for Dear Mr. Henshaw.
3. What she wants to give her readers. (3 words)
4. The state where she was born.
5. The company that publishes her books.
6. The city where she grew up.
7. The city where she worked in the Public Library.
8. The things she told her husband she needed in order to write a book.
9. The state where she lives today
10. Most people think she has a ----- -- -----. (3 words)
11. Her first profession.
12. Her birthday month.
13. The town where she lived as a pre-schooler.

Crossword #4: Ramona

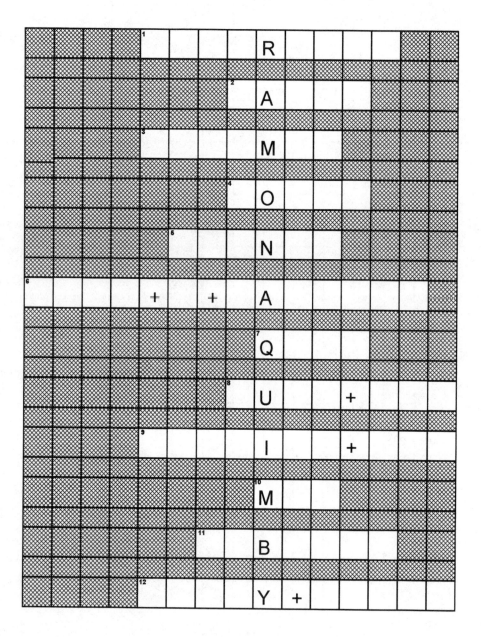

ACROSS CLUES

1. One of Ramona's dolls.
2. An imaginary lizard.
3. After wearing these under her shirt and slacks, Ramona left them at school.
4. Ramona's friend.
5. Miss _____, kindergarten teacher.
6. Picky-Picky eats this instead pf Puss-Puddy.
7. Beezus and Ramona urge their father to ____ smoking.
8. Mother's sister.
9. A favorite TV star.
10. When Ramona is stuck in this, Henry rescues her.
11. Ramona's baby sister.
12. The Quimby cat.

Crossword #5: Maggie & Socks

ACROSS CLUES

5. The Brickers bought Socks outside a _____
7. What Maggie refused to learn.
9. What Maggie delivers.
10. Sock's family
11. Socks grew fat on this.
12. A word to describe Maggie.
13. Why Maggie changed her mind.
15. The color of Sock's feet
19. A kind man who helped Maggie.
20. The fat cat's menu
22. Socks's rival for the Brickers' love.
23. A disapproving grandparent.

DOWN CLUES

1. The Brickers spent lots of time on this.
2. Socks's feelings when he became an outside cat.
3. Charles William's toy.
4. Mrs. Riley was a kind _____.
6. An understanding teacher.
7. Maggie's writing tool.
8. How Socks felt about the new baby.
14. Maggie's grade in school.
15. A hairpiece, not a toy.
16. What Charles William and Socks became.
17. Mrs. Bricker's way into her baby's room.
18. Socks's type of cat.
21. Old Taylor.

From *The Beverly Cleary Handbook*. © Teacher Ideas Press. (800) 237-6124.

Crossword #6: Ellen Tebbits

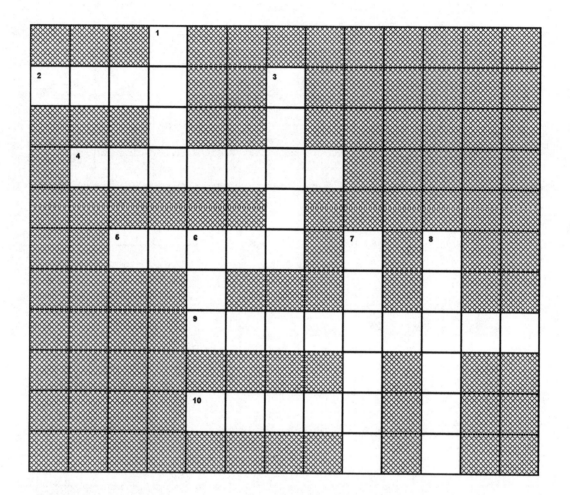

ACROSS CLUES

2. The biennial Ellen brought to school.
4. Ellen's best friend.
5. Ellen pretended she knew all about this.
9. The street where Ellen lives.
10. The teacher's name is Miss . . . . .

DOWN CLUES

1. NOT Ellen's friend.
3. Lessons she takes at Spofford's.
6. Ellen is cast as a substitute one.
7. Fun to clean by clapping.
8. Uncomfortable underwear.

Crossword #7: Ralph

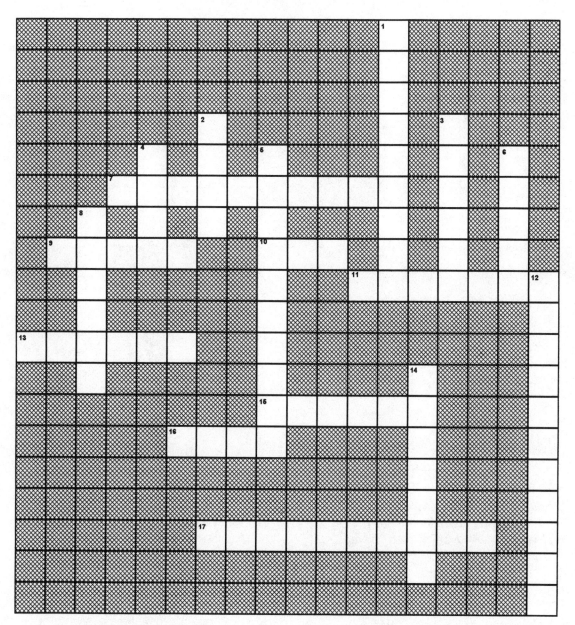

ACROSS CLUES

7. Home of the Mountain View Inn.
9. Ralph's friend.
10. Ralph's deadly enemy.
11. The type of dog in 211.
13. Matt's description of Ralph.
15. A dirty trap for Ralph.
16. Escape route to the first floor.
17. A garage for the motorcycle.

DOWN CLUES

1. Emergency aspirin transporter.
2. Keith's home.
3. Ralph's uncle.
4. The bellman.
5. Ralph's pride and joy.
6. Keith thought Ralph was _____.
8. Headgear for a cyclist.
12. Growing up means learning to be this.
14. Fever-breaker.

Crossword #8: Ramona Again

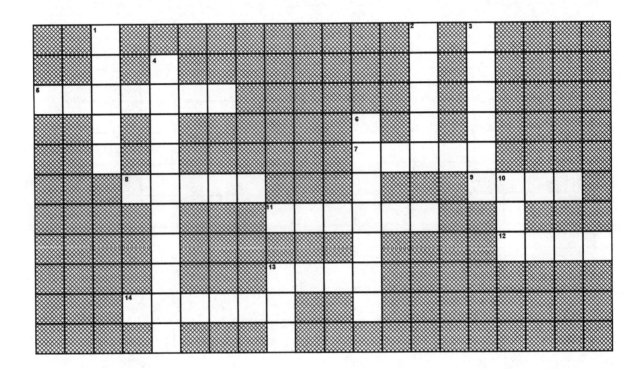

ACROSS CLUES

5. Beezus's favorite teacher.
7. A temporary name for the baby.
8. Ramona, with a black nose, played one of these.
9. Ramona's joyful world.
11. A word to describe Ramona.
13. Where Ramona found a wedding ring.
14. Howie made two pair of these from coffee cans.

DOWN CLUES

1. A crown of these gets tangled in hair.
2. What Susan's curls say to Ramona.
3. Ramona's third grade teacher.
4. She always wanted to squeeze out all of this at once.
6. A star spangled light.
10. What is raw and in Ramona's hair?
13. Ramona's favorite time at school.

Crossword #9: Strider

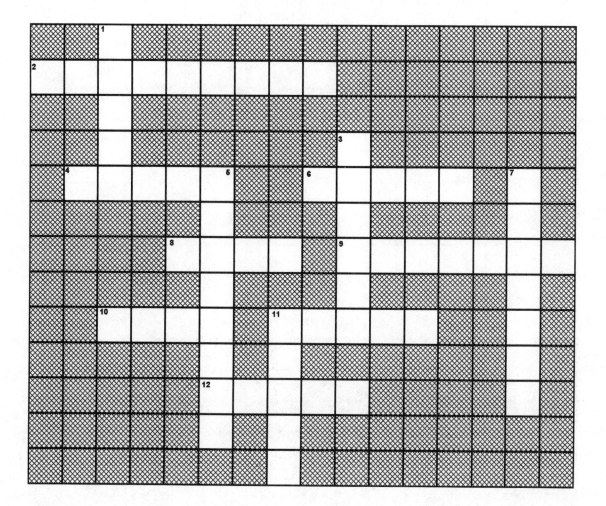

ACROSS CLUES

2. A beach guardian.
4. Leigh made a date to pull _____.
6. A running friend.
8. An unusual skill for a dog.
9. Wounded-Hair taught this.
10. Brinkerhoffs throw spagetti on this.
11. Where Strider was found.
12. Mom studies to be one.

DOWN CLUES

1. Dad helped Leigh build this.
3. A running redhead.
5. The landlady.
7. Strider was held in joint _____.
11. Half owner of Strider.

Crossword #10: Emily

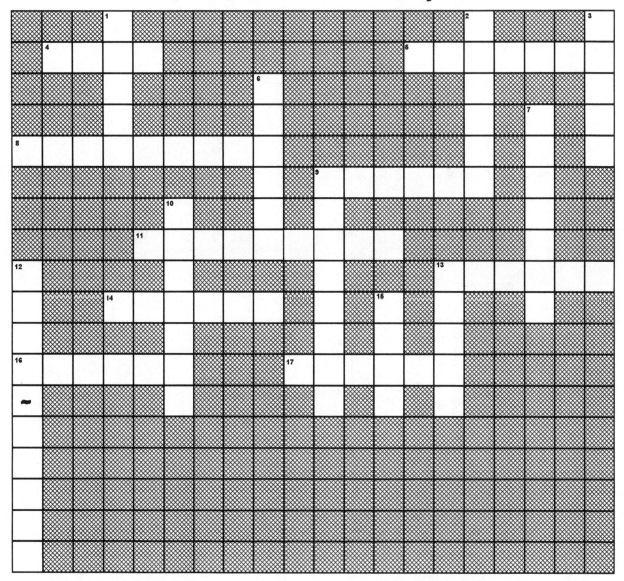

ACROSS CLUES

4. Emily's prize money bought a _____.
5. A wave from one is a thrill.
8. What Emily gave Fong Quock.
9. A new name for the old dog.
11. Emily's hometown.
13. How to clean up an old horse.
14. Emily's cousin.
16. Emily's prize money
17. The state where Emily lives.

DOWN CLUES

1. Fong Quock's gift to the library.
2. Grandpa bought a Tin _____
3. Emily wore her best one to the hard-times party.
6. Emily thought she's been traded for one.
7. A kind of pie for a pot luck.
9. Emily's ancestors.
10. Mama started one.
12. A party for poor folks.
13. Fonk Quock's homeland.
15. Tipsy guests at a fancy luncheon.

Crossword #11: Otis

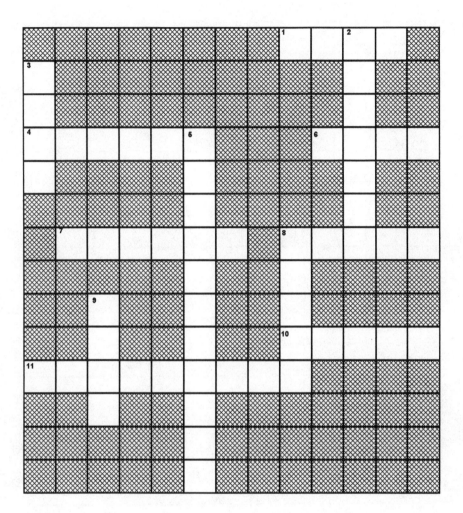

ACROSS CLUES

1. An underfed white rat.
4. When Otis chewed this, Ellen held her nose.
6. Otis gets into trouble when he is cast as the front half of one of these.
7. Otis's teacher is Mrs. _____.
8. Otis's friend.
10. Not Otis's friend.
11. Otis chewed paper to make these.

DOWN CLUES

2. Stirring this up makes Otis happy.
3. A collection of 30 of these saves a football game.
5. Mrs. Gitler is sure Otis will get this someday.
8. Ellen and Austine made off with Otis's _____.
9. Make sure you only cut your own.

Crossword #12: Mitch & Amy

ACROSS CLUES

3. Amy brought Mitch a book about Wild Bill _____.
4. Alan dared Mitch to a game of _____.
6. The new girl in class and Scouts.
10. Mitch's class searched for this in water at a Savings and Loan.
11. Mitch and Amy do it a lot.
12. Alan wanted to ruin the whole box of these.

DOWN CLUES

1. Mitch built his own and Alan broke it.
2. Amy and her friends like to belong to _____.
3. Amy plays cello, Mitch plays a _____.
5. Amy helped Mitch build this out of toothpicks.
8. Amy and Mitch, the Huff _____.
9. Mitch has a hard time with this.

Selections for Further Reading

BEVERLY CLEARY'S CHILDHOOD FAVORITES

In *A Girl from Yamhill*[1] and in several published interviews,[2] Mrs. Cleary names the books she most enjoyed when she was young. Following is a list of these books, for those who might be interested in comparing her childhood reading with the books she later produced. Nearly all these titles are out-of-print, but many can still be found in libraries and accessed through library systems. Only those titles accessible through library system records are listed here.

Books That Were Read Aloud to Her

Jacobs, Joseph. *English Fairy Tales*. Illustrated by John D. Batten. New York: Putnam, [n.d.].
　　These humorous tales are appealing in format and illustration and are remarkable for the number that are suitable for young children.

MacDonald, George. *The Princess and Curdy*. New York: Macmillan, 1964, c1954.

———. *The Princess and the Goblin*. New York: Morrow, 1986.
　　These stories tell of a little princess and her friend Curdy, who protects the princess from goblin miners who live beneath her castle.

Maeterlink, Maurice. *The Blue Bird: Fairy Play in Six Acts*. New York: Dodd, 1965, c1911.
　　Two children set off in search of the blue bird of happiness, experiencing amazing adventures during their quest.

Potter, Beatrix. *The Tailor of Gloucester*. New York: Warne, 1987, c1903.
　　A tailor is commissioned to produce a waistcoat for the mayor. When the tailor becomes sick, mice come to his rescue and complete the coat for him.

Books That She Read by Herself

Alcott, Louisa May. *Little Women*. New York: Grossett, 1990, c1947.
A timeless story about a family of four teenage girls who live during the United States Civil War. This warm, loving family group struggles with individual problems and poverty but is sustained by love for each other. Many editions are available.

Barrie, James M. *Peter Pan*. New York: Holt, 1987.
The classic story of Peter, Wendy, Tinkerbell, and Captain Hook. Many editions are available.

Bennett, Ethel Hume. *Camp Ken-jockety*. Boston: Houghton, 1923.

Lofting, Hugh. *The Story of Doctor Doolittle: Being the History of His Peculiar Life at Home and Astonishing Adventures in Foreign Parts: Never Before Printed*. New York: Lippincott, 1920.
This story tells of a kind-hearted doctor who travels through Africa attempting to cure monkeys of a terrible illness. Doctor Doolittle has the ability to understand the language of animals.

Perkins, Lucy Fitch. *The Dutch Twins*. New York: Walker, 1968, c1911.
Kit and Kat skate on the canal, celebrate St. Nicholas Day, shop at the village market, and fish off the pier.

———. *The Swiss Twins*. New York: Walker, 1969, c1922.
Seppi and Leneli, who live in a chalet in the mountains of Switzerland, encounter an avalanche.

Twain, Mark [pseud. for Samuel Clemens]. *The Adventures of Tom Sawyer*. New York: Harper & Row, 1876. First published in 1876 and 1855.
Here are funny and sometimes hair-raising adventures of Tom and his pal Huck growing up in a small river town in the mid-1800s.

Rankin, Carroll (Watson). *Dandelion Cottage*. New York: Holt, 1983, c1904.
One of the Dandelion series.

Snedeker, Caroline Dale (Parke). *Downright Dencey*. New York: Doubleday, Page & Co., 1927.
A friendship develops between a little Quaker girl and a waif she thoughtlessly injured on Nantucket Island at the beginning of the nineteenth century.

Spyri, Johanna. *Heidi*. New York: Ariel Books/Knopf, 1984.
The classic tale of a young girl who lives in the Swiss Alps with her grandfather. Many editions are available.

Webster, Jean. *Daddy Long-Legs*. New York: Grossett, 1964, c1940.
An orphan in a boarding school meets the wealthy guardians she has corresponded with for many years.

BOOKS BY BEVERLY CLEARY

Beezus and Ramona. Illustrated by Louis Darling. New York: Morrow, 1955. (See page 10.)

Dear Mr. Henshaw. Illustrated by Paul O. Zelinski. New York: Morrow, 1983. (See page 29.)

Ellen Tebbits. Illustrated by Louis Darling. New York: Morrow, 1951, 1979. (See page 25.)

Emily's Runaway Imagination. Illustrated by Beth Krush and Joe Krush. New York: Morrow, 1961. (See page 39.)

Fifteen. Illustrated by Joe Krush and Beth Krush. New York: Morrow, 1956. (See page 43.)

A Girl from Yamhill: A Memoir. New York: Morrow, 1988. (See page 47.)

The Growing Up Feet. Illustrated by DyAnne DiSalvo-Ryan. New York: Morrow, 1987. (See page 36.)

Henry and Beezus. Illustrated by Louis Darling. New York: Morrow, 1952. (See page 8.)

Henry and Ribsy. Illustrated by Louis Darling. New York: Morrow, 1954. (See page 9.)

Henry and the Clubhouse. Illustrated by Louis Darling. New York: Morrow, 1962. (See page 12.)

Henry and the Paper Route. Illustrated by Louis Darling. New York: Morrow, 1957. (See page 11.)

Henry Huggins. Illustrated by Louis Darling. New York: Morrow, 1950, 1978. (See page 7.)

Hullabaloo ABC. Illustrated by Earl Thollander. Berkeley, California: Parnassus, 1960. (See page 37.)

Janet's Thingamajigs. Illustrated by DyAnne DiSalvo-Ryan. New York: Morrow, 1987. (See page 37.)

Jean and Johnny. Illustrated by Joe Krush and Beth Krush. New York: Morrow, 1959. (See page 44.)

Leave It to Beaver. New York: Berkeley, 1960.

Beaver and Wally. New York: Berkeley, 1961.

Here's Beaver. New York: Berkeley, 1961.
    These three books are based upon episodes in the television series by Joe Connelly and Bob Mosher.

The Luckiest Girl. New York: Morrow, 1958. (See page 45.)

Lucky Chuck. Illustrated by J. Winslow Higginbottom. New York: Morrow, 1984. (See page 37.)

Mitch and Amy. Illustrated by George Porter. New York: Morrow, 1967. (See page 41.)

The Mouse and the Motorcycle. Illustrated by Louis Darling. New York: Morrow, 1965. (See page 32.)

Muggie Maggie. Illustrated by Kay Life. New York: Morrow, 1990. (See page 42.)

My Own Two Feet: A Memoir. New York: Morrow, 1995. (See page 47.)

Otis Spofford. Illustrated by Louis Darling. New York: Morrow, 1953. (See page 27.)

Petey's Bedtime Story. Illustrated by David Small. New York: Morrow, 1993. (See page 38.)

Ralph S. Mouse. Illustrated by Paul O. Zelinsky. New York: Morrow, 1982. (See page 35.)

Ramona and Her Father. Illustrated by Alan Tiegreen. New York: Morrow, 1975, 1982. (See page 18.)

Ramona and Her Mother. Illustrated by Alan Tiegreen. New York: Morrow, 1979. (See page 19.)

Ramona Forever. Illustrated by Alan Tiegreen. New York: Morrow, 1984. (See page 22.)

Ramona Quimby, Age 8. Illustrated by Alan Tiegreen. New York: Morrow, 1981. (See page 21.)

Ramona the Brave. Illustrated by Alan Tiegreen. New York: Morrow, 1975. (See page 16.)

Ramona the Pest. Illustrated by Louis Darling. New York: Morrow, 1968. (See page 15.)

The Real Hole. Illustrated by Mary Stevens. New York: Morrow, 1960. (See page 38.)

Ribsy. Illustrated by Louis Darling. New York: Morrow, 1964. (See page 14.)

Runaway Ralph. Illustrated by Louis Darling. New York: Morrow, 1970. (See page 33.)

Sister of the Bride. Illustrated by Beth Krush and Joe Krush. New York: Morrow, 1963. (See page 46.)

Socks. Illustrated by Beatrice Darwin. New York: Morrow, 1973. (See page 42.)

Strider. Illustrated by Paul O. Zelinsky. New York: Morrow, 1991. (See page 30.)

Two Dog Biscuits. Illustrated by Mary Stevens. New York: Morrow, 1961. (See page 38.)

Two Dog Biscuits. Illustrated by DyAnne DiSalvo-Ryan. New York: Morrow, 1986.

SHORT STORIES AND PLAYS BY BEVERLY CLEARY

"Dad, Do You Love Me?" *Redbook* (November 1983): 50-60.
    Excerpted from the Sunday, February four entry from Leigh's diary in *Dear Mr. Henshaw.*

"Josie Lays Her Down to Sleep." *Woman's Day* (February 5, 1984): 36ff.
    This short story tells of a six-year-old who witnesses the violence on the television news. Josie goes to bed fearful of saying her prayers because they contain the phrase "If I should die before I wake." Each night, Josie is afraid that she will not live to see the next day. She tries to stay awake, sometimes falling into sleep filled with nightmares. There is no happy resolution to this story, only a subtle indictment of television violence and parents who do not truly listen to their children.

The Sausage on the End of the Nose. New York: Children's Book Council, 1974.
    This short play with a cast of 12 was written for Book Week. The action takes place in a school library where many popular children's books have come to life. Homer Price, Paddington, Ramona, Mary Poppins, and others bemoan the rough treatment they have received at the hands of careless readers. A book called *Fairy Tales* has a sausage on the end of its nose because a girl was reading the *Three Wishes* but had to return to class and could not finish the story. The sausage will remain until someone reads the ending of the tale. A boy wanders into the library and announces that he really does not like to read, but his teacher has ordered him to check out a book. The books conspire to have him solve Fairy Tale's sausage problem, and then they entice him into checking out that book and reading the end of the tale. He checks out and *A Bear Called Paddington,* too.
    It is interesting to note that Cleary's first impetus toward a writing career came when she was in seventh grade—her school librarian gave the assignment of writing an essay about a favorite book character. Unable to decide among her favorites, Beverly wrote about a girl who went to Bookland and talked to book characters who had come to life. The librarian later read the essay aloud to the class and suggested that Cleary should become an author of children's books when she grew up. She was excited and intrigued, but her mother suggested that she think of a way of earning a living that would provide a steady source of income while she wrote. Beverly thought that the next best thing to being a writer would be a career as a librarian, and with that, the decision was made.[3]

NONFICTION ARTICLES BY BEVERLY CLEARY (ARRANGED CHRONOLOGICALLY)

"Writing Books About Henry Huggins." *Top of the News* 24 (December 1957): 7–11.
    Mrs. Cleary gave this talk at the Pacific Northwest Library Association (PNLA) conference in 1957 when *Henry and Ribsy* was the winner of the PNLA Young Reader's Choice Award. She tells the story of the beginnings of the Yamhill Public Library and of her delight in finding a large public library when she moved to Portland. She describes the books she enjoyed as a child and the selection criteria she developed at that time. She tells of the seventh-grade incident during which a teacher told her that she should someday write books for children, and how she instead trained to be a librarian. The events leading up to the writing of *Henry Huggins* and *Henry and Ribsy* are described.

"1960 Reader's Choice Award Acceptance." *PNLA Quarterly* 25 (April 1961): 175–76.

This acceptance letter was written for the 1960 PNLA conference when *Henry and the Paper Route* was the winner of the Reader's Choice Award. In it she describes how she gathered incidents from her experience until she had enough material to write a story, and how she had to write the book an hour at a time while her one-year-old twins took their morning naps.

"Low Man in the Reading Circle: Or A Blackbird Takes Wing." *Horn Book* 45 (June 1969): 287–93.

This speech was given by Mrs. Cleary when she received the William Allen White Children's Book Award, and again when she won the Pacific Northwest Young Reader's Choice Award. Both events occurred in 1968, and both awards were for *The Mouse and the Motorcycle*. Here she tells, for the first time, how she struggled to learn to read. She recounts her disgust with her primary reading textbooks and how she thought reading was not fun until she discovered a book that was easy enough to read by herself—and funny and exciting to boot. She describes her concern and empathy for her son who, was baffled by the reading process just as she had been. *The Mouse and the Motorcycle* was written for him after an incident in an old British Inn and the sight of a mouse trapped in a neighbor's bucket came together to form the nucleus of a story.

"On Talking Back to Authors." *Claremont Reading Conference Yearbook* 34 (1970): 1–11.

Cleary tells the story of her struggle with learning to read and of her disgust with the children's books that were popular during her youth, books that often contained the instructional interjections of the author. She tells how she longed for books about real children like the ones she knew. She discusses trends in children's books, the letters she receives from children, and her hope of being able to write books that will help children discover that reading can be fun.

"How Long Does It Take to Write a Book?" *Oklahoma Librarian* 21 (July 1971): 14–17.

Ramona the Pest was the recipient of the Sequoyah Children's Book Award in 1971, and Cleary wrote this article in response to that honor. The title of the article refers to a question she is often asked. Cleary recounts her frustration as a student whenever she had an assignment with a required length. She tells of her mother inspiring a love of stories, but of cruel teachers and dull textbooks dashing her desire to learn to read. She tells of her desire to write the kind of books she wanted to read as a child, discusses the circumstances surrounding the creation of Ramona in the first Henry Huggins book, and details the way Ramona became the central figure of a book many years later.

"Writing Without Stretch." *PNLA Quarterly* 36 (October 1971): 23–24.

In 1971, *Ramona the Pest* was chosen as the winner of the PNLA Young Reader's Choice Award. This letter to the association is Cleary's response to that award. Essentially, this letter excerpts a previous article by Cleary, "How Long Does It Take to Write a Book?"

"Laura Ingalls Wilder Award Acceptance." *Horn Book* 51 (August 1975): 361–64.

Cleary discusses her pioneer ancestors, the hardships they faced, her parents and their struggle for economic survival, and her difficult childhood. She explains how these influences contribute to the books she writes for the children of today.

"1980 Regina Recipient (Acceptance Speech)." *Catholic Library World* 52 (July 1980): 22–26.

In this acceptance speech, Cleary discusses the year she spent as a children's librarian in Yakima, Washington and how her experiences of trying to find good books for reluctant readers influenced her writing style. She reflects on 30 years of changes—changes in society and changes in books. She cites many letters received from children that caused her concern. There are interesting sidelights of textbook publishers wanting to change her material before including it in reading textbooks. In revealing passages, she discusses stereotypes of children's books and the pressure on writers to be "with it" when creating works of contemporary fiction.

"The Laughter of Children." *Horn Book* 58 (October 1982): 555–64.

This is a glimpse of the artist and craftswoman behind the funny stories. Cleary discusses the elements of humor in her books, why children find them funny, and the value of humor to a child intent on growing up. Of particular interest is her description of the child within her, for whom she writes.

"Acceptance Statement." *Claremont Reading Conference Yearbook* 47 (1983): 89–90.

In her acceptance statement for the George S. Stone Center for Children's Books Recognition of Merit Award, Cleary tells of her concern for the children who experience insecurity and sadness as family unity is threatened. She comments that, as a child, she turned to reading for comfort, and that, as an adult, she writes the kind of books she wanted to read as a child—books that might bring some pleasure and solace to children.

"Newbery Medal Acceptance." *Horn Book* 60 (August 1984): 429–38.

Cleary's talk opens with a tribute to her mother as her first and best teacher. Much of her writing style she attributes to her early training by her mother. She goes on to describe the disturbing changes in letters received from children, who demand things from her—answers to their questions or material items—expressing a dark and lonely side of childhood. Cleary discusses her discouragement with children who become bored if a task requires any effort, but also the encouragement of knowing that many children turn to books, even if for comfort in times of stress. She discusses the impetus for writing *Dear Mr. Henshaw* and tells of the reactions she received from children who read the book.

"Why Are Children Writing to Me Instead of Reading?" *New York Times,* November 10, 1985, 42.

Cleary recounts her childhood and adult dislike of the intrusion of an author's voice into a book. She explains that she can neither understand nor justify the letters from children who ask her trivial questions that have no connection to her books.

"Dear Author, Answer This Letter Now . . ." *Instructor* 95 (November/December 1985): 22–23+.

In this open letter to teachers, Cleary discusses the disturbing trends in letters received from children who read her books.

ARTICLES AND BOOKS ABOUT BEVERLY CLEARY AND HER WORK

"After Forty Years, Kid-Lit Queen Beverly Cleary's Gentle Tales Are Turning Up on Television." *People Weekly* 30 (October 3, 1988): 59–60.

In this interview, Cleary mentions the changes in letters received from readers. Cleary explains her belief that, despite their superficial sophistication, people still want the same things from life. The interview includes photos of Cleary and her husband.

"Beverly Cleary: A Practicing Perfectionist." *Early Years* 13 (August/September 1982): 24–25+.

This article touches upon Cleary's home and family. During the interview portion, Cleary discusses her work ethic, her views on young people, and offers tips for teachers. The article includes photos of Cleary and her husband.

"Beverly Cleary." *Children's Literature Review* VIII (1985): 44–51.

Excerpts of reviews (published up to 1985) of Cleary's books.

Burns, Paul C., and Ruth Hines. "Beverly Cleary: Wonderful World of Humor." *Elementary English* 44 (November 1967): 743–47+.

This examination of Cleary's work contains brief excerpts from her letters to Burns and Hines.

Chatton, Barbara. "Ramona and Her Neighbors: Why We Love Them." *Horn Book* 71 (May/June 1995): 297–304.

This chronological study of Henry and Ramona discusses how Cleary's Oregon stories provide a picture of the changes in middle-class American life and in educational methods during the previous 40 years.

Churchman, Deborah. "Children's Literature: A Source of Hope and Morality." *Christian Science Monitor* (June 6, 1983): 17.

A discussion of contemporary children's literature, with Julius Lester, Lloyd Alexander, Lois Lowry, and Beverly Cleary.

"Cleary Donates Bookmobile Gift." *Wilson Library Bulletin* 68 (September 1993): 18.

A news report on Cleary's donation, including a photo of the author and her gift.

Cooper, Ilene. "Popular Reading—After Henry Huggins." *Booklist* 83 (November 1, 1986): 415–16.

A list of books similar to *Henry Huggins* that boys might enjoy.

Cooper, Ilene. "The Booklist Interview." *Booklist* 87 (October 15, 1990): 448–49.

In this interview, Cleary discusses the effect of television on children's literature and the writing of her autobiography *A Girl from Yamhill*.

Epstein, Connie C. "Beverly Cleary: An Outstanding Children's Author." *Catholic Library World* 51 (February 1980): 274–75.

A broad look at Cleary, covering her background, her work, and the honors she has received.

Fitzgibbons, Shirley. "Focus on Beverly Cleary." *Top of the News* (winter 1977): 167–70.
In this interview, Cleary states that, as a child, she was much like Ellen Tebbits, and that her personal favorite among her books (at the time of this interview) is *Emily's Runaway Imagination.* Cleary offers her views on trends in children's literature.

Frederick, Heather Vogel. "And to Think That I Saw It on Klickitat Street." *Publishers Weekly* 240 (October 11, 1993): 31.
History behind the Grant Park project in Portland.

Hansen, Sandra. "Henry, Beezus, Ribsy and Beverly." *Writer's Digest* (January 1983): 20–21.
Cleary discusses on the "new realism" in children's books and makes some interesting comments on *Fifteen.*

Hauser, Susan G. "Ramona the Pest in Brass." *Wall Street Journal*, November 15, 1995, A20.
A humorous look at Cleary by a fellow graduate of Fernwood School along with an account of the Grant Park Sculpture Garden project.

Herron, Celia. "Cleary Thinks Books Should Be Fun." *Christian Science Monitor* (May 14, 1982): B6.
In this interview, Cleary mentions that Ramona has the same feelings as she did as a child, and again blames television for today's superficially sophisticated children.

Hopkins, Lee B. "Beverly Cleary." In *More Books by More People.* New York: Citation Press, 1974.
A brief biography, an interview, and a review of several Cleary books.

Lalley, Heather. "Portland Memorializes Favorite Little Girl: Ramona Quimby, Larger Than Life." *Oregonian*, October 14, 1995, C1+.
An account of the dedication of the Beverly Cleary Sculpture Garden for Children.

Malkey, Margaret. "Ramona the Chronotype: The Young Reader and Social Theories of Narrative." *Children's Literature in Education* 22 (June 1991): 97–110.
An essay on the use of story to shape the perceptions of time and space—Cleary's observations of childhood and the skill with which she shapes those observations into story in turn shape her reader's perceptions of their own lives.

Martin, Patricia Stone. *Beverly Cleary: She Makes Reading Fun.* Vero Beach, FL: Rourke, 1987.
This brief biography designed for young people highlights Cleary's reading problems as a child and her resulting desire to produce children's books that are fun to read. Information on goal-setting techniques is included.

Nist, J. S. "Popularity in Wonderland." Paper presented at the annual meeting of the Popular Culture Association in the South, Jacksonville, Florida, October 1977.
Nist argues that those who are specialists in children's literature and award prizes should look to the books that children themselves choose to read. Nist uses the Henry Huggins series as an example of popular books overlooked in prestigious awards.

Novinger, Margaret. "Beverly Cleary: A Favorite Author of Children." *Southeastern Librarian* 18 (fall 1968): 194–202. Reprinted in *Authors and Illustrators of Children's Books*, edited by Mirium Hoffman and Eva Samuels. New York: R. R. Bowker, 1972.
A critical analysis of Cleary's work up to 1972. "Mrs. Cleary may be called the Boswell of the average child."

Paterson, Katherine. "Ramona Redux." In *Gates of Excellence: On Reading and Writing Books for Children.* New York: Nelson, 1981.
This distinguished author writes an especially perceptive review of *Ramona and Her Father.*

Pflieger, Pat. *Beverly Cleary.* Boston: Twayne, 1991.
This book contains critical reviews of Cleary's works taken from a wide variety of sources. A chronology and bibliography are included.

Rahn, Suzanne. "Cat-Child: Rediscovering Socks & Island McKenzie." *The Lion and the Unicorn* 12 (1988): 111–20.
A discussion of the traditional role of cats in children's literature and an analysis of *Socks* in relationship to that role.

Rees, David. "Middle of the Way: Rodie Sudbery and Beverly Cleary." In *The Marble in the Water.* Boston: Horn Book, 1980.
An essay on writers who are popular with children but who do not often receive critical acclaim. Rees uses Cleary's works to illustrate quality literature that is overlooked.

Reichenbach, Jean. "Beverly Cleary." *Columns: The University of Washington Alumni Magazine* 13 (September 1993): 41.
An interview during which Cleary recalls her days as a student at the University of Washington library school.

Reuther, David. "Beverly Cleary." *Horn Book* 60 (August 1984): 439–43.
Cleary's editor writes about the author as she is honored with the Newbery Award for *Dear Mr. Henshaw.*

Roggenbuck, Mary June. "Profile: Beverly Cleary—The Children's Force at Work." *Language Arts* 56 (January 1979): 55–60.
A discussion of Cleary's work, including comments from Cleary's letters to Roggenbuck.

Sanders, Maureen. "Literacy as a 'Passionate Attention.' " *Language Arts* 64 (October 1987): 619–33.
A detailed observation of one child's reaction to the Ramona series to see how this child brings her own meaning to literacy activities.

Scott, Elaine. *Ramona: Behind the Scenes of a Television Show.* New York: Dell, 1988.
An entertaining photo essay that introduces young people to the intricacies of television production using as background the 10-part Public Broadcasting System series on Ramona Quimby. There are many informal pictures of Mrs. Cleary and interesting facts about the casting and production of the series. This is a good companion to the video tapes that are often used in classrooms as motivation for reading.

Zarrille, James. "Beverly Cleary, Ramona Quimby and the Teaching of Reading." *Children's Literature Association Quarterly* 12 (1988): 131–35.
An examination of the processes by which Ramona learns to read and the lessons to be learned from her books. This article shows how the Ramona books can be used as instructional materials for reading teachers.

ADDITIONAL BIOGRAPHICAL SOURCES

"Beverly Cleary." In *Something About the Author*, vol. 43, edited by Anne Commire. Detroit: Gale, 1986.

"Beverly Cleary." In *Contemporary Authors: New Revision Series*, vol. 19. Detroit: Gale, 1987. "Cleary, Beverly (Atlee Bunn) 1916–".
Includes interview.

"Beverly Cleary." In *Contemporary Authors: New Revised Series*, vol. 36. Detroit: Gale, 1992. "Cleary, Beverly (Atlee Bunn) 1916–"
Includes recent bibliography of Cleary's work.

NOTES

1. Beverly Cleary, *A Girl from Yamhill: A Memoir* (New York: Morrow, 1988), 62, 73, 92–93, 124.

2. Beverly Cleary, "Writing Books About Henry Huggins," *Top of the News* 24 (December 1957): 7–9.

3. Beverly Cleary, *A Girl From Yamhill: A Memoir* (New York: Morrow, 1988), 145–47.

Appendix:
Keys for Independent Activities
(Chapter 4)

FIND THESE STORY PLACES (p. 93)

1. 7 (In all Henry and Ramona books to *Ramona Quimby, Age 8*)
2. 6 (*Henry and Ribsy*)
3. 1 (*Otis Spofford*)
4. 2 (*Ramona Quimby, Age 8*)
5. 9 (*Henry Huggins* and *Henry and the Paper Route*)
6. 10 (*Ramona and Her Father*)
7. 15 (*Otis Spofford* and *Ellen Tebbits*)
8. 8 (*Beezus and Ramona*)
9. 4 (*Henry and the Paper Route*)
10. 3 (*Ramona Forever*)
11. 5 (*Ramona the Pest*)
12. 12 (Grant Park, Portland, OR)

FIND THE STREET (p. 93)

1. Klickitat Street (All Henry and Ramona books)
2. Knott Street (*Henry and the Paper Route*)
3. Tillamook Street (*Ellen Tebbits*)
4. Lombard Street (*Henry and the Clubhouse*)
5. Any two of the following: The Columbia River, Mt. Hood, Interstate Bridge, Glenwood School (*Ramona and Her Father*)

HIDDEN NAMES (p. 94)

1. Most people think this book has a sw<u>ell end</u>ing. <u>ELLEN</u>

2. She preferred handkerchiefs t<u>o tis</u>sues. <u>OTIS</u>

3. Weight lifting can <u>be a tricep</u>s builder. <u>BEATRICE</u>

4. How many kids can c<u>ram on a </u>bus? <u>RAMONA</u>

5. I like my ham sandwiches best w<u>hen rye</u> bread is used along with swiss cheese. <u>HENRY</u>

6. In the new shopping mal<u>l, eigh</u>ty stores proudly opened their doors. <u>LEIGH</u>

7. When the girls waded in the creek, they took off their shoes and <u>socks</u>. <u>SOCKS</u>

8. Texas A & M college students call their football tea<u>m "Aggie</u>s." <u>MAGGIE</u>

9. He spent an hou<u>r alph</u>abetizing animals. <u>RALPH</u>

10. I told th<u>em! I, ly</u>ing here, have the chicken pox! <u>EMILY</u>

SCRAMBLED TITLES (p. 95)

1. *Emily's Runaway Imagination*

2. *Socks*

3. *Ribsy*

4. *Henry Huggins*

5. *Otis Spofford*

6. *Ramona Quimby, Age 8*

7. *Ramona the Brave*

8. *Henry and Ribsy*

9. *The Mouse and the Motorcycle*

10. *Ellen Tebbits*

TURNING FACTS INTO FICTION (p. 100)

    _5_   *Ramona the Brave*, chapter 3

    _4_   *Ramona and Her Father*, chapter 1

    _6_   *Otis Spofford*, chapter 2

    _____   *Ramona the Brave*, chapter 5

    _3_   *Beezus and Ramona*, chapter 4

    _2_   *Beezus and Ramona*, chapter 2

MORE FACTS/MORE FICTION (p. 101)

    4   *Ramona Quimby, Age 8*, chapter 3

    6   *Ellen Tebbits*, chapter 4

    3   *Ramona the Pest*, chapter 2

    2   *Ramona and Her Father*, chapter 5

    _____   *Henry and Ribsy*, chapter 2

    7   *Ramona the Pest*, chapter 3

    5   *Ellen Tebbits*, chapter 1

    _____   *Ramona and Her Mother*, chapter 5

    1   *Ramona the Pest*, chapter 8

MUGGIE MAGGIE (p. 103)

Muggie Maggie is about a girl who is in the **third** grade. She doesn't want to learn to write in **cursive**. Her teacher, Mrs. Leeper, sent her to the school office to talk to the **principal**. Maggie was made **message** monitor. She carried **notes** to other teachers. She couldn't read the **notes** until she learned to read **cursive**. She practiced at home and soon was able to read and write **cursive**, and she could read the **notes,** too. When she read a **note** written by the principal, she found that it was about her!

BEEZUS AND RAMONA (p. 104)

Answers will vary.

SOCKS (p. 105)

Answers will vary.

RIBSY (p. 106)

ACTION	WORKED	USELESS
1. Ribsy jumped out of the Dingley's car and ran away, still smelling like violets.		X
2. Henry placed an advertisement in the paper for a lost dog.	X	
3. Ribsy followed a mailman onto a bus.		X
4. Ribsy chased a squirrel around a classroom.		X
5. Ribsy played in a high school football game.	X	
6. Henry telephoned Joe Saylor.	X	
7. Ribsy ran away from Joe, looking for Henry.		X
8. Ribsy taught Larry how to play ball.	X	
9. Henry and his family drove around looking for Ribsy.	X	
10. Ribsy barked and barked when he was caught on the fire escape.		X

HENRY AND THE CLUBHOUSE (p. 107)

Answers will vary.

RUNAWAY RALPH (p. 108)

1. Ralph can't get his motorcycle down the front steps of the Inn.   Ralph
2. Ralph is chased by Sam, who tries to keep him out of Happy Acres Camp.   gopher
3. Catso uses Ralph to teach the kittens how to terrorize a mouse.   Garf
4. Ralph was lonely in his cage and wanted someone to talk with.   Chum
5. Ralph was locked in a cage and had to escape.   Catso
6. Garf has the motorcycle, and Ralph wants it back.   Ralph
7. Ralph can't drag Karen's watch to her sleeping bag.   Sam
8. Ralph must return to the Mountain View Inn before winter comes.   Garf

DEAR MR. HENSHAW (p. 109)

Answers will vary but the address on the postcard is:

Leigh Botts
(students may leave this line blank or make up an appropriate street address)
Pacific Grove, California 90406

RALPH S. MOUSE (p. 111)

Designs will vary.

RAMONA AND HER MOTHER (p. 112)

Answers will vary.

REBUSES

Page 114—Beverly Cleary

Page 115—Ramona Quimby

Page 116—Klickitat Street

Page 117—Runaway Ralph

Page 118—Henry Huggins

Crossword Key #1: Ribsy

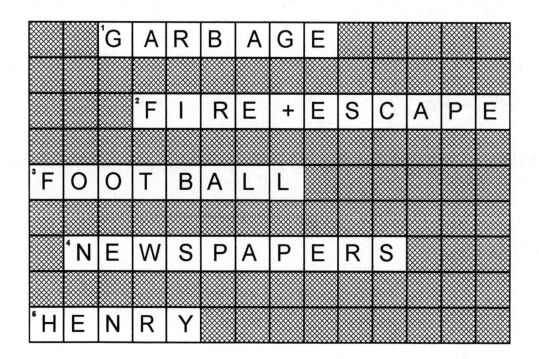

Word List:

FIRE+ESCAPE
FOOTBALL
GARBAGE
HENRY
NEWSPAPERS

Crossword Key #2: Henry

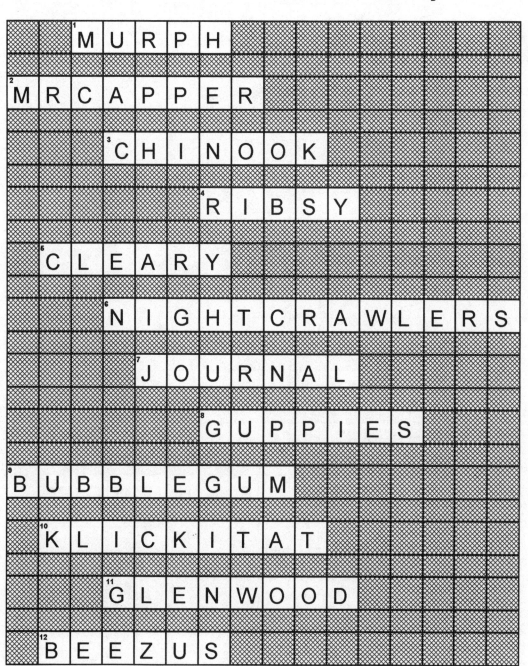

Word List:

1. BEEZUS
2. BUBBLEGUM
3. CHINOOK
4. CLEARY
5. GLENWOOD
6. GUPPIES
7. JOURNAL
8. KLICKTAT
9. MRCAPPER
10. MURPH
11. NIGHTCRAWLERS
12. RIBSY

Crossword Key #3: The Author

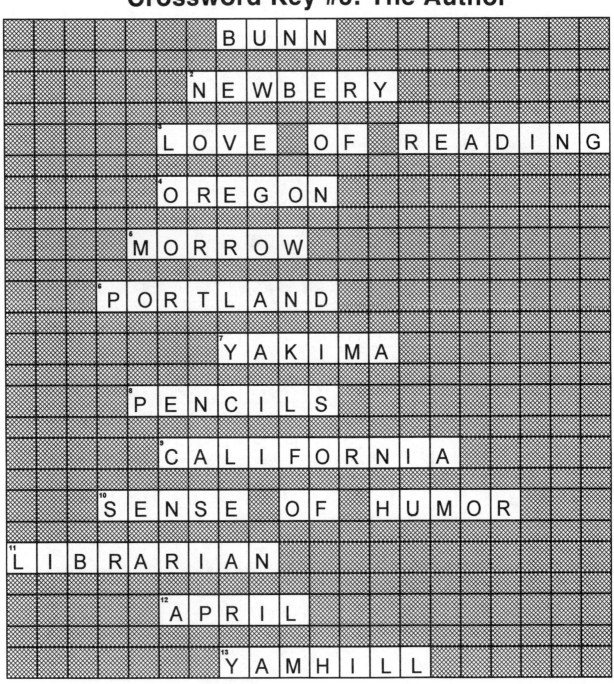

Word List:

1. APRIL
2. BUNN
3. CALIFORNIA
4. LIBRARIAN
5. LOVE OF READING
6. MORROW
7. NEWBERY
8. OREGON
9. PENCILS
10. PORTLAND
11. SENSE OF HUMOR
12. YAKIMA
13. YAMHILL

Crossword Key #4: Ramona

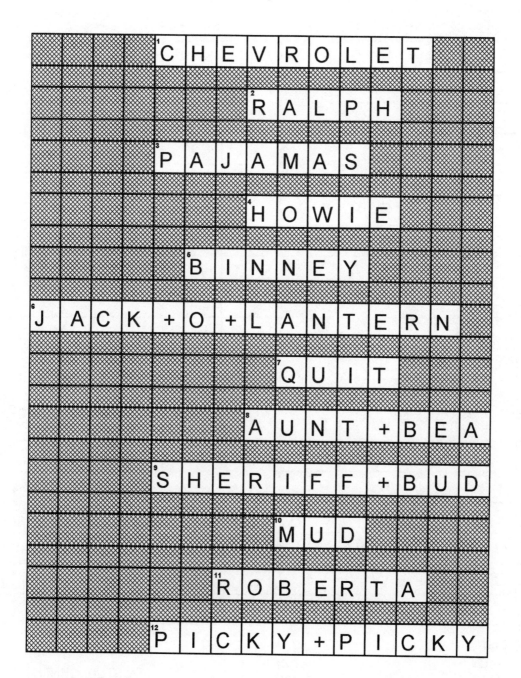

Word List:

1. AUNT BEA
2. BINNEY
3. CHEVROLET
4. HOWIE
5. JACK O LANTERN
6. MUD

7. PAJAMAS
8. PICKY PICKY
9. QUIT
10. RALPH
11. ROBERTA
12. SHERIFF BUD

Crossword Key #5: Maggie & Socks

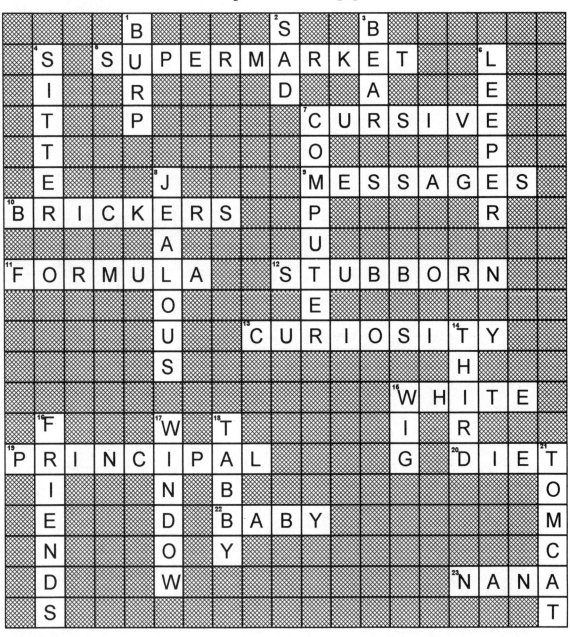

Word List:

1. BABY
2. BEAR
3. BRICKERS
4. BURP
5. COMPUTERS
6. CURIOSITY
7. DIET
8. FORMULA
9. FRIENDS
10. JEALOUS
11. LEEPER
12. MESSAGES
13. NANA
14. PRINCIPAL
15. SAD
16. SITTER
17. STUBBORN
18. SUPERMARKET
19. TABBY
20. THIRD
21. TOMCAT
22. WHITE
23. WIG
24. WINDOW

Crossword Key #6: Ellen Tebbits

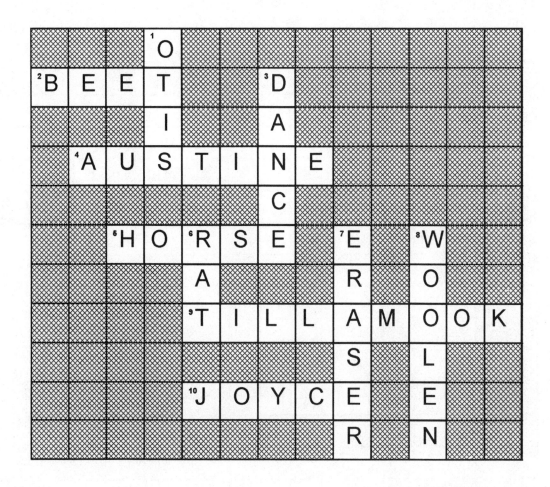

Word List:

AUSTINE	HORSE	RAT
BEET	JOYCE	TILLAMOOK
DANCE	OTIS	WOOLEN
ERASER		

Crossword Key #7: Ralph

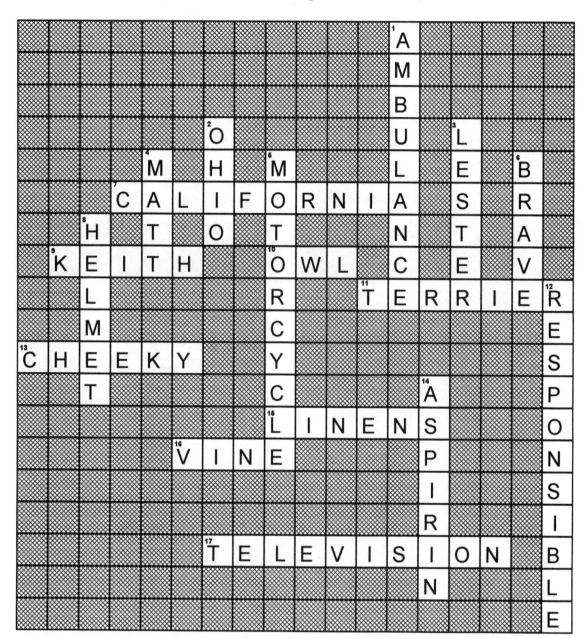

Word List:

AMBULANCE
ASPIRIN
BRAVE
CALIFORNIA
CHEEKY
HELMET

KEITH
LESTER
LINENS
MATT
MOTORCYCLE
OHIO

OWL
RESPONSIBLE
TERRIER
TELEVISION
VINE

Crossword Key #8: Ramona Again

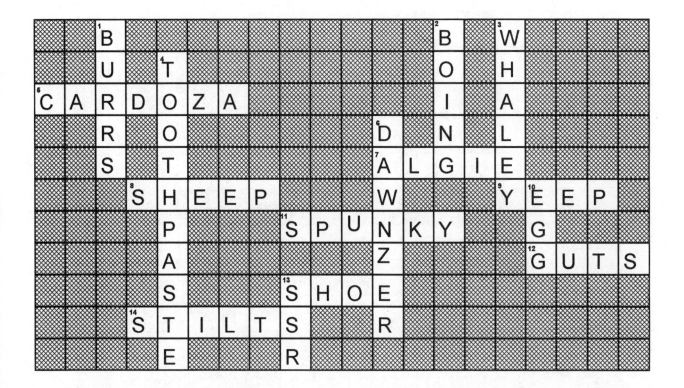

Word List:

ALGIE
BOING
BURRS
CARDOZA
DAWNZER
EGG
GUTS
SHEEP

SHOE
SPUNKY
SSR
STILTS
TOOTHPASTE
WHALEY
YEEP

Crossword Key #9: Strider

```
        ¹F
²P R E S I D E N T
   N
   C                    ³G
⁴W E E D S⁵      ⁶K E V I N        ⁷C
        M        N              U
       ⁸R E A D  ⁹E N G L I S H
        R        V              T
   ¹⁰W A L L ¹¹B E A C H        O
        I    A                 D
       ¹²N U R S E              Y
        G    R
             Y
```

WORD LIST

BARRY
BEACH
CUSTODY
ENGLISH
FENCE
GENEVA

KEVIN
NURSE
PRESIDENT
READ
SMERLING
WALL
WEEDS

Crossword Key #10: Emily

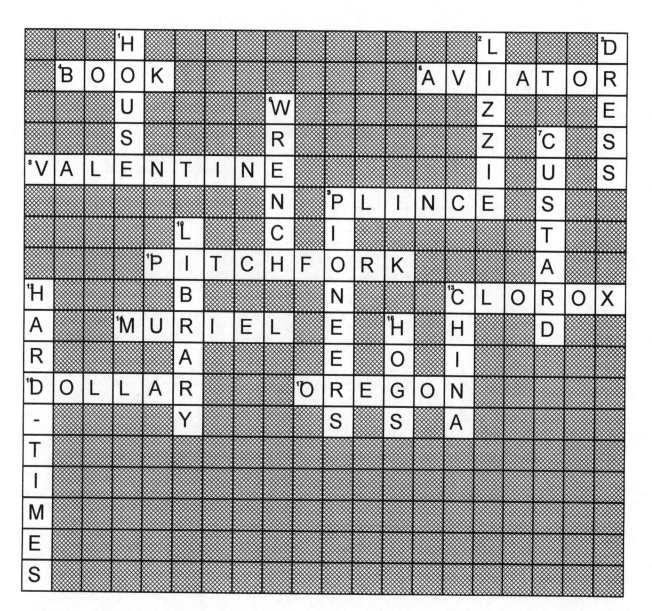

Word List:

AVIATOR	HARD-TIMES	OREGON
BOOK	HOUSE	PITCHFORK
CHINA	HOGS	PIONEERS
CLOROX	LIZZIE	PLINCE
CUSTARD	LIBRARY	VALENTINE
DOLLAR	MURIEL	WRENCH
DRESS		

Crossword Key #11: Otis

						¹M	U	T	²T	
³B									R	
U									O	
⁴G	A	R	L	I	⁵C			⁶B	U	L	L
S					O				B	
					M				L	
⁷G	I	T	L	E	R		⁸S	T	E	W	Y
					U			H		
		⁹H			P			O	
		A			P		¹⁰E	L	L	E	N
¹¹S	P	I	T	B	A	L	L	S	
		R			N			
					C			
					E			

Word List:

BULL
BUGS
COMEUPPANCE
ELLEN
GARLIC
GITLER

HAIR
MUTT
SHOES
SPITBALLS
STEWY
TROUBLE

Crossword Key #12: Mitch & Amy

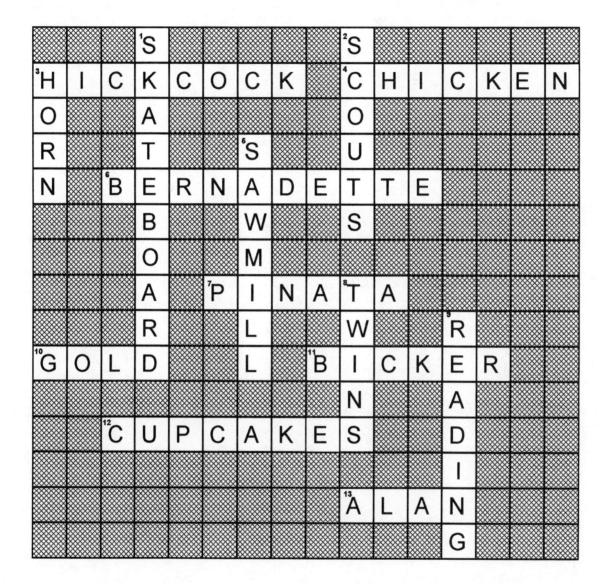

Word List:

ALAN
BERNADETTE
BICKER
CHICKEN
CUPCAKES
GOLD
HICKOCK

HORN
PINATA
READING
SAWMILL
SCOUTS
SKATEBOARD
TWINS

Index

American Book Award for Children's Fiction, 20

Banks, Oregon, 1
Beaumont Middle School, 56–57
Beezus and Ramona, 47, 104
Berkeley, California, 4, 46, 61, 71
Beverly Cleary Sculpture Garden for Children, 62, 139
Boston Globe Horn Book Honor Book, 19
Bunn, Lloyd, 1–3, 51–52, 60
Bunn, Mabel Atlee, 1–3, 45–46, 51–52

Carmel, California, 5, 61
Chaffee Junior College, 4, 47, 60
Charlie May Simon Award, 34
Christopher Award, 30
Cleary, Clarence T., 4, 48, 61
Cleary, Malcolm, 5, 32–33, 41–42, 61
Cleary, Marianne, 5, 32, 41, 61
Commonwealth Silver Medal, 30

Darling, Louis, 7–12, 14–15, 25, 27, 32–33, 35
Darwin, Beatrice, 42
Dear Mr. Henshaw, 61–62, 68, 71, 109, 137, 140
DiSalvo-Ryan, DyAnne, 36–38
Dorothy Canfield Fisher Memorial Children's Book Award, 15, 30, 44

Ellen Tebbits, 6, 49, 56, 67, 71, 124
Emily's Runaway Imagination, 2, 51, 71, 128, 139

Fernwood School, 2, 3, 51–54, 139
Fifteen, 139
"Friends of Henry and Ramona", 62, 139

Garden State Children's Award, 19, 20, 22, 30, 42
Georgia Children's Award, 16
Girl From Yamhill, 1, 39, 45, 100–101, 138
Golden Archer Award, 18, 43
Grant Park, Portland, Oregon, 51, 62, 139
Great Stone Face Award, 33

Hawaii Association of School Librarians Honor Book, 30
Henry and Ribsy, 55, 135
Henry and the Clubhouse, 65, 107
Henry and the Paper Route, 57–58, 136
Henry Huggins, 5, 48, 51, 55, 58, 61–62, 118, 135
Henry Huggins books, 49, 71, 120, 138–39
Higgenbottom, J. Winslow, 37
Hollywood Theater, Portland, OR, 57
Horn Book Honor List, 30
Hunt, Lee, 62

International Board on Books for Young People Honor List, 19
Iowa Children's Choice Award, 25

Klickitat Street, Portland, Oregon, 52, 55–56, 62, 116
Krush, Beth and Joe, 39, 43, 44, 46, 56

Land of Enchantment Award, 19
Laura Ingalls Wilder Award 5, 136
Laurelhurst Park, 58
Laurelhurst School, 59
Life, Kay, 42
Luckiest Girl, The, 47, 71

Mark Twain Award, 18
Massachusetts Award, 30
McMinnville, Oregon, 1, 22, 51
Michigan Young Reader's Award, 22
Mitch and Amy, 2, 61, 71, 130
Monterey County, California, 5
Mouse and the Motorcycle, The, 62, 71, 125, 136
Muggie Maggie, 103, 123

Nene Award, 15–16, 19, 33–34
New England Round Table Honor Award, 7
New York Times Notable Book Award, 25, 30
Newbery Award, 5, 19, 22, 30, 62, 137, 140

Oakland, California, 4
Ontario, California, 3–4
Otis Spofford, 2, 6, 49, 56–58, 66–67, 71, 129

Pacific Grove, California, 29, 61–62, 68, 71
Pacific North West Library Association Young Reader's Choice Award, 10, 12, 16, 19, 33, 135–36
Parent's Choice for Literature Award, 25, 30
Porter, George, 41
Portland, Oregon, 2, 5, 6, 39, 49–60, 62, 71, 92

Ralph S. Mouse, 62, 71, 111
Ramona and Her Father, 6, 60, 140
Ramona and Her Mother, 6, 112
Ramona Quimby, Age 8, 54, 56, 59
Ramona the Pest, 54, 136
Ramona Quimby books, 2, 6, 49, 71, 115, 122, 126, 136
Reading Magic Award, 32
Regina Award, 5, 137
Ribsy, 106, 119
Rose City Branch Library, Portland, 3, 51, 53
Runaway Ralph, 62, 71, 108, 117

Sausage on the End of the Nose, 3
School Library Journal Honor List, 30
Seattle, Washington, 4
Sequoyah Children's Book Award, 16, 30, 136
Sister of the Bride, 61, 71
Small, David, 38

Socks, 62, 140, 105, 123
Stevens, Mary, 38
Strider, 61, 68, 71, 127
Sue Hefley Award, 33
Surrey School Award, 20, 33

Texas Bluebonnet Award, 19
Thollander, Earl, 37
Tiegreen, Alan, 16, 18–19, 21–22

University of California at Berkeley, 4, 46, 60–61
University of Washington, Seattle, 4, 60, 140
Utah Children's Choice Award, 19

Volunteer Award, 19

William Allen White Award, 33, 43, 136
World War II, 4, 61

Yakima, Washington, 4, 60, 137
Yamhill, Oregon, 1–3, 39, 51, 56, 71

Zelinsky, Paul O., 29–30

About the Author

Joanne Kelly has had an active and avid interest in children's literature since she haunted Chicago's school and public libraries during her childhood. Her previous books, *Newbery Authors of the Eastern Seaboard*, *The Battle of Books*, *On Location*, and *Rebuses for Readers* (in collaboration with Pat Martin and Kay V. Grabow), have drawn upon her depth of knowledge about good plots, settings, and characters in books for young people, but she has long had an interest in the real places where stories happen. She has a B.S. in elementary education, an M.S. in library science, and a certificate of advanced study in library science, all from the University of Illinois. She served as an elementary librarian for 24 years and as coordinator of the district libraries of the Urbana School District, Urbana, Illinois, for 9 years. She and her husband Chuck live in Champaign, Illinois. When Chuck is not taking pictures for Joanne's books, he is occupied as head of Engineering, Office of Instructional Resources, University of Illinois at Urbana-Champaign.

About the Illustrator

Pat Martin has earned bachelor's and master's degrees from the University of Illinois at Urbana-Champaign and is employed as an art coordinator at Publication Services in Champaign. Previously, during the time that her two children attended Thomas Paine Elementary School in Urbana, Pat volunteered in the library where Joanne Kelly was the librarian. Pat's work at the library provided her with an excellent outlet for her interest in children's literature and art. When her children went on to junior high school, Pat taught undergraduate mathematics at the University of Illinois at Urbana-Champaign, where she served for 7 years. At the same time that Pat began training for a career in graphic arts, Joanne Kelly began writing teacher resource books, which she asked Pat to illustrate. *The Beverly Cleary Handbook* is the fifth book on which they have collaborated.

from *Teacher Ideas Press*
/Libraries Unlimited

NEWBERY AUTHORS OF THE EASTERN SEABOARD:
Integrating Social Studies and Literature, Grades 5–8

Take students on an exciting learning journey where they explore the roads, towns, homes, landscapes, and eras of their favorite books and authors. Focusing on works of Cynthia Voigt, Elizabeth George Speare, Katherine Paterson, and Marguerite Henry, this fascinating book describes the settings of these authors' works and provides related activities that make literature and the history behind it come alive. Projects encourage learning in social studies, history, and geography. Loaded with photographs, maps, drawings, and reading lists, this resource offers a wealth of material for the upper elementary and junior high classroom. A great supplement for literature classes, social studies, and author studies—this is truly a treasure for anyone who loves children's books! **Grades 5–8.**

ix, 159p. 8½x11 paper ISBN 1-56308-122-9

ON LOCATION: Settings from Famous Children's Books

An outstanding learning opportunity for children...The Sterling North Society recommends On Location as a resource for teachers <u>and</u> parents.—**The Rascal**

Recommended pick...It's a fine way of learning about places which form the settings from famous children's books.—**Bookwatch**

Watch youngsters enthusiasm grow as they discover the church belfry where Poe-the-Crow lived, the bluff where Caddie Woodlawn and her brothers picked blueberries, and many other intriguing places from Laura Ingalls Wilder's *Little House in the Big Woods*, Marion Dane Bauer's *On My Honor*, Carol Ryrie Brink's *Caddie Woodlawn* and *Magical Melons*, Sterling North's *Rascal*, and Irene Hunt's *Across Five Aprils*. Engaging selections and a variety of geography and extension activities—accompanied by attractive and detailed maps, drawings, and photographs—build student knowledge of geography, literature, history, social studies, math, and science. **Grades 3–8.**

xv, 129p. 8½x11 paper ISBN 1-56308-023-0

THE BATTLE OF BOOKS: K–8

The book offers ideas for combining battles with thinking skills; written skits for a number of the books; and numerous reproducible certificates, bookmarks, and display ideas.—**Library Talk**

Thinking skills are sharply honed here in a style kids love.—**Reference Desk**

Use this famous game as a reading promotion or as a fun activity for the classroom. Kelly provides more than 800 questions arranged by book type (classics, award books, popular, contemporary novels, and so on). Battles can be graded according to the ability levels of students. **Grades K–8.**

xiii, 201p. 8½x11 paper ISBN 0-87287-779-5